Contents

Introduction

Welcome, and thank you for being someone who reads introductions. It gives me the chance to introduce the book you are about to read as a compilation of ideas and activities that I have gleaned during a lifetime of teaching. It also contains some of the best practices of teachers with whom I have had the pleasure of working.

This book is intended for teachers, especially those who teach in middle school or junior high. It is an introduction to essay writing, a book that will help teachers help students write better essays. Although I have not taught at the high-school level, I believe that this book might be of assistance to many teachers there as a review of the basics—just don't expect it to be the "go to" source for the upper grade levels.

I have written this book in the way that I would want one written to help me if I were still in the classroom. The sequence is basically the one that I used during the latter years of my career—start at the beginning and continue until the parade is over. Included are notes and exercises for students, explanations of what has worked (and what hasn't worked) for me, and tips for teaching particular concepts. I hope my asides shed light on the business of teaching, not just the essay, but many of the prerequisites to essay writing. Within each chapter, the material is presented as lessons. And because I wanted to make this resource as user-friendly as possible, reproducible forms and templates for assignments or notes have been placed within each of the lessons.

Students often do not understand why they have to write essays. Middle-school students ask if it is to acquire a skill needed in high school ("Preparation H" syndrome); high-school students believe it's a skill required in college. As teachers, our task is to foster inquiring minds. The skills required to write an essay are the same skills required to write a speech, to prepare a persuasive argument, to prove a point, to explain an idea—and on the list goes. If we can help our students acquire these skills as we "teach" the essay, we will have assisted them in accomplishing truly valuable life skills. In my experience (a phrase often repeated in the pages that follow), essays have a bad reputation among students. If we can teach essay writing in a way that engages and challenges them, we can change their opinions about essays and writing.

Poet Donald Hall once said, "The best writing is like the letter O. But the writer only writes the letter C. It is the reader who fills the gap with his or her own experience." I am not suggesting that this book is the "best writing." I am suggesting that once you have read it, a task remains. Your task, dear reader, is to fill in the gaps for your students. Massage the information to suit your needs, mold the materials so that they are appropriate for your classes, and make it your own.

Best wishes.

1 What Is an Essay?

The only place where "success" comes before "work" is in the dictionary.

I start with this quote for the simple reason that some of what we need to know about essays is not particularly entertaining. It might even seem like work. Hang in there; it gets better.

Defining the Essay

M.H. Abrams notes that the essay is "Any short composition in prose that undertakes to discuss a matter, express a point of view, or persuade us to accept a thesis on any subject."

For me, the essay has always been a thing for teaching in the spring. I see the planning, researching, and writing of an essay as a major project. A variety of prerequisite skills—idea gathering, topic narrowing, topic sentence and paragraph writing, and more—are required. As the months from September to February or March pass, I try to build the anticipation toward the opportunity for essay writing. I think about how Tom Sawyer convinced his friends to whitewash Aunt Polly's fence:

> "…I reckon there ain't one boy in a thousand, maybe two thousand, that can do it the way it's got to be done."

That's how I try to make essay writing—a task worthy of care, attention, and anticipation.

Although how you actually define an essay will depend on you and your class, you will probably want to cover the following in a very basic way:

- the purpose of an essay
- the basic structure of an essay
- how the essay structure fulfills the purpose
- types of essays
- what an essay is not

When the time finally arrives, I use cloze notes to reinforce how we, as a class, have defined the essay. I believe that cloze notes take the drudgery out of note taking, provide the essential skeleton for tidy notes, reinforce the key elements of what is being studied, and show students that you are using note taking for a reasonable, helpful purpose and not just to give yourself an extended coffee break.

The Defining the Essay: Cloze Exercise on page 8 has blanks for students to fill in; the completed version on page 9 can be used as an overhead projection.

Teaching Tip
• Note that the very first idea in the cloze exercise underscores the notion that an essay is an *opportunity* that allows a student to choose a topic of personal interest and the challenge to explain it to others.

The Shape of the Essay

For many of today's students, an essay is five to seven paragraphs of prose writing that explains or persuades. The actual length of the body of the essay is not particularly relevant. What is important is that students understand the general overview of the essay.

I like to begin with a picture. My students know that I promote visualization, so it doesn't come as a surprise to most of them that I have a Picture of an Essay (page 10) up my painter's smock.

In class, I just draw a bunch of lines on the board. As this is a teacher reference, I jazzed up my artistic rendition to create what you see on page 10—but the essence is the same. I take students through my Picture step-by-step.

For another example of a visual tool, see the Picture of a Paragraph on page 54 and the formula for a topic sentence (page 55).

1. The introductory paragraph is relatively short. On a classroom whiteboard I draw my lines in green to symbolize *Go*. It is the beginning and invites the reader to proceed. The concluding paragraph—in red to symbolize *Stop*—is also quite short.
2. The body paragraphs are longer than either the introduction or conclusion. The left margins are as straight as an arrow, as a teacher's path to the coffee machine, or as a Sunday-school teacher's sense of humor. While the right margins are as crooked as a dog's hind leg, a politician's promise, or a principal's path to the point he is trying to make, they are straight enough to centre the writing as would a picture frame. Arrows join the paragraphs, showing that the preceding one is connected to the latter.
3. The sentences in blue on my classroom whiteboard are the topic sentences. Topic sentences, in individual paragraphs, will have been taught earlier in the year and in previous grades. When I am drawing and coloring the essay picture, I will remind students of the concept of a topic sentence, but won't dwell on it until we look at some exemplars (see pages 56–57).

Teaching Tips
• I often draw an arrow from the concluding paragraph back to the introduction because the "cyclic return" is such a common technique.
• When hyphens are included, I use this opportunity to give a mini-lesson on syllabication.
• See page 56 if your students need a lesson on varying positions for the topic sentence.

Defining the Essay: Cloze Exercise

Name: _____

An essay is an opportunity to _____

and to _____ .

In its most basic form, an essay is five _____ written about

_____. One paragraph _____ the topic, three body

paragraphs tell _____, and the final paragraph acts as a

_____ .

An essay is a series of paragraphs where you :

_____,

then you _____,

and then you _____.

An essay is "any short composition in prose that undertakes to

• discuss a matter,

• _____,

• or _____ (main idea)

on any subject."

What an essay is not:

• an _____ —a longer piece found in a newspaper or magazine

• a _____ —an account or a statement of facts

• a _____ —"Hey, essay, how's it goin'? Whassup?"

Defining the Essay: Cloze Completed

An essay is an opportunity *to find out about a topic of interest to you* and to *explain it to a reader*.

In its most basic form, an essay is five *paragraphs* written about *a topic of your choice.* One paragraph *introduces* the topic, three body paragraphs tell *about the topic*, and the final paragraph acts as a *conclusion.*

An essay is a series of paragraphs where you:

Tell 'em what you're gonna tell 'em,

then you *Tell 'em,*

and then you *Tell 'em what you told 'em.*

An essay is "any short composition in prose that undertakes to

- discuss a matter,
- *express a point of view,*
- or *persuade us to accept a thesis* (main idea)

on any subject."

What an essay is not:

- an *article*—a longer piece found in a newspaper or magazine
- a *report*—an account or a statement of facts
- a *greeting*—"Hey, essay, how's it goin'? Whassup?"

Picture of an Essay

Green green green, green green green green green green green green green: Green green green green green green green green green green green. Green — green — green, green! Green green green green, green green green green. Green green green green, green green green green green green green green. Green green green green green-green. Green green green, green green green.

Blue blue blue blue blue blue blue blue blue blue blue blue blue blue blue. Ηε τοοκ ηισ ϖορπαλ σωορδ ιν ηανδ. Λονγ τιμε τηε μανξομε φοε ηε σουγητ Σο ρεστεδ -ουσε βψ τηε Τυμτυμ τρεε, ανδ στοοδ αωηιλε ιν εψεσ οφ φλαμε, Χαμε — ωηιφφλινγ τηρουγη τηε τυλγεψ ωοοδ,Ανδ βυρβλεδ ασ ιτ χαμε. Ονε — τωο. Ονε, τωο! Ανδ τηρουγη ανδ τηρουγη Τηε ϖορπαλ βλαδε ωεντ σνιχκερ–σναχκ. Ηε λεφτ ιτ δεαδ, ανδ ωιτη ιτσ ηεδ Ηε ωεντ γαλυμπηινγ βαχκ. Ονε — τωο. Ονε, τωο! Ανδ τηρουγη ανδ τηρουγη Τηε ϖορπαλ βλαδε ωεντ σνιχκερ–σναχκ! Ηε λεφτ ιτ δεαδ, ανδ ωιτη ιτσ ηεαδ Ηε ωεντ γαλυμπη–ιγ βαχκ.

Ανδ, ηασ τηου σλαιν τηε θαββερωοχκ? **Blue blue blue blue blue: blue blue blue blue.** Χομε το μψ αρμσ, μψ βεαμιση βοψ. Ο φραβφουσ δαψ! Χαλλοοη! Χαλλαψ! ηεχηορτλεδ ιν ηισ φοψ. Τωασ βριλλιγ, ανδ τηε σλιτηψ τοϖεσ. Διδ γψρε ανδ γιμβλε ιν τηε ωαβε; αλλ μιμσψ ωερε τηε βορογοϖεσ, ανδ τηε μομε ρατησ ουτγραβε. Ιτ ωασ βριλλ– ιγ, ανδ τηε σλιτηψ τοϖεσ διδ γψρε ανδ γιμβλε ιν τηε ωαβε: Αλλ μιμσψ ωερε τηε– βορογοϖεσ ανδ τηε μομε ρατησ ουτγραβε. Βεωαρε τηε θαββερωοχκ, μψ σον. Τηε φαωστηατ βιτε, τηε — χλαωσ τηατ χατχη. Βεωαρε τηε θυβφυβ βιρδ, ανδ σηυν τηε φρυμιουσ Βανδερσνατχη. Αλλ — μιμσψ ωερε τηε βορογοϖεσ ανδ τηε μομε ρατησ ουτγραβε. Βεωαρε τηε θαββερωοχκ, μψ σον.

Ηε τοοκ ηισ ϖορπαλ σωορδ ιν ηανδ. Λονγ τιμε τηε μανξομε φοε ηε σουγητ Σο ρεστεδ ηε βψ τηε Τυμτυμ τρεε, ανδ στοοδ αωηιλε ιν τηουγητ. Ανδ, ασ ιν υφφιση τηουγητ ηε στοοδ,Τηε θαββερωοχκ, ωιτη εψεσ οφ φλαμε, Χαμε ωηιφφλινγ τηρουγη τηε τυλγεψ ωοοδ,Ανδ βυρβλεδ ασ ιτ χαμε. Ονε, τωο. Ονε, τωο. Ηε χηορτλεδ ιν ηισ φοψ. Τωασ βριλλιγ, ανδ τηε σλιτηψ τοϖεσ. Διδ γψρε ανδ γιμβλε ιν τηε ωαβε. Ανδ τηρουγη ανδ– τηρουγη Τηε ϖορπαλ βλαδε ωεντ σνιχκερ–σναχκ. Ιτ ωασ βριλλιγ, ανδ τηε σλιτηψ τοϖεσ διδ γψρε ανδ γιμβλε ιν τηε ωαβε: Αλλ μιμσψ ωερε τηε βορογοϖεσ ανδ τηε– μομε ρατησ ουτγραβε. Βεωαρε τηε θαββερωοχκ, μψ σον. Τηε φαωσ τηατ βιτε, τηε χλαωσ τηατ χατχη! Ηε λεφτ ιτ δεαδ, ανδ ωιτη ιτσ ηεαδ Ηε ωεντ γαλυμπηινγ βαχκ. **Blue blue blue blue blue blue blue blue blue blue blue blue blue blue blue blue blue**

Red, red red red red red red red red red red? Red red red red, red red red — red! Red red red red! Red Red! Red red red red red red red red red. Red red, red red red red red red red red. Red red red red red red red red; red red red red red red red red red, red red red red red red red. Red red red red red red red red. Red red, red red red red red red red red. Red red red red red red red red; red red red red red red red, red red red red red red red red.

Acting Out an Essay

Borrow the Social Studies people for a few minutes to act as an audience; they need a break from all of that High Vocabulary-Low Interest stuff, or at least from trying to learn from history that we really *can* learn from history.

Realists in the reading audience might predict a problems with the pinkie touching; but it does work, even if just for the actual performance period.

Not only do I share a picture of an essay with my students, I have also tried *acting out* an essay. It can take all of the students in a class to perform "The Essay," so it is best to invite another class and seat them in the desks.

My invigorated Language Arts students ring the room.

1. Each student represents a sentence. Each group of students represents a paragraph. The last person in each group/paragraph (except the concluding one) holds out an arm and hooks pinkie fingers with the first person in the adjacent group/paragraph (except the introductory one). This symbolizes the connection between paragraphs.
2. The "topic sentences" do something (point to themselves, do a little dance) to distinguish themselves from the other people in their groups/paragraphs.
3. Members of the introductory paragraph do something to draw attention to themselves. Gestures—such as turning and motioning with upturned palms—toward the groups that follow underscore the essence of the introductory paragraph: to arouse interest and explain what is to follow.
4. The members of the concluding paragraph can combine the "time out" hand signal with singing a little "Da da ta da Roo do da do do do" and pointing to the introductory paragraph. They are saying, "Stop, that's all there is folks," and reminding the audience of the cyclic-return concept.

The possibilities are endless. Is it possible to show that quotes have been used? Can you indicate order, unity, clarity? What other visual and vocal variations can be included? Get the picture?

Teaching Tips
- The first and last groups/paragraphs contain fewer students, reflecting how the introductory and concluding paragraphs are usually shorter.
- Make sure that the "topic sentences" are not all positioned at the beginning of their groups.
- Performances of "The Essay" are recommended at a midpoint as well as at the end of this unit. You will be amazed at the growth.
- By introducing the idea that an essay can be acted out, you open the door to challenging students to incorporate other aspects of essay writing into further performances.
- Different variables—students of varying heights, the addition of sound effects, etc.— can be used, not only to show what is laudable about a good essay, but what should be avoided in a "not-so-good" essay.

The Essay Outline

Once I have shared the Picture of an Essay (page 10) and the class has "acted out" an essay (page 11), I leave the note taking about essays for several days. As Li'l Abner said, "Too much is more than enough." I turn to

- possible topics of interest
- narrowing topics for individual essays (see pages 18–19)
- practising with the form of an outline (see pages 37–38)
- a first look at research (see pages 43–48)

I then return to the big picture and present the Essay Outline (page 13), bringing together all the aspects listed above, and how they relate to the essay.

Teaching Tips

- Have the students do the cloze notes in outline form, using the Essay Outline: Cloze Exercise on page 14.
- This is a good time to introduce the essay title page.
- The back of the title page can be used as a checklist, for the student and/or teacher to keep a running account of the progress of the essay.

Essay Outline

TITLE

I.   Introductory paragraph

    A. Gets the reader's attention (captures his/her interest)

    B. Tells the reader what to expect in the essay

    C. Is usually shorter than the body paragraphs

II. Body Paragraph #1

    A. Often begins with a topic sentence

    B. Explains one of three major points about the topic

    C. Might contain reasons and examples

    D. Is linked to the following paragraph

III. Body Paragraph #2

    A. Might have the topic sentence as the second sentence

    B. Discusses a second major point about the topic

    C. Might contain quotations and statistics

    D. Is linked to the following paragraph

IV. Body Paragraph #3

    A. Might have the topic sentence as the last sentence

    B. Discusses the last major point about the topic

        1. The last point is often the most important point.

        2. The other paragraphs may have been building toward this one.

    C. Might contain opinions and personal stories

    D. Is linked to the following paragraph

V.   Concluding paragraph

    A. Usually begins with a word or phrase that signals the ending

    B. Lets the reader know that the essay is over

        1. Like *THE END* in a children's book, it signals the end.

        2. If it is done well, the reader would never turn the page.

    C. Is frequently shorter than the body paragraphs

Essay Outline: Cloze Exercise

Name: _____

_____

___. _____ paragraph

   ___. Gets the _____ (captures his/her interest)
   ___. Tells the reader _____ in the essay
   ___. Is usually _____ than the body paragraphs

___. Body Paragraph #1

   ___. Often begins _____
   ___. Explains one of three _____ about the topic
   ___. Might contain _____
   ___. Is linked to the following paragraph

___. Body Paragraph #2

   ___. Might have the topic sentence as the _____ sentence
   ___. Discusses a second major point _____
   ___. Might contain _____
   ___ Is linked to the following paragraph

___. Body Paragraph #3

   ___. Might have _____ as the last sentence
   ___. Discusses the last major point about the topic
      ___. The last point is often the _____ point.
      ___. The other _____ may have been building toward this one.
   ___. Might contain _____
   ___. Is linked to the following paragraph

___. Concluding paragraph

   ___. Usually begins with a word or phrase that _____
   ___. Lets the reader know that the essay is _____
      ___. Like _____ in a children's book, it signals the end.
      ___. If it is done well, the reader would never _____.
   ___. Is frequently _____ than the body paragraphs

2 First Things First

Beware: Don't be a member of the "Ready, Shoot, Aim" club.

Things to teach before teaching the essay:
- formal and informal writing
- creativity
- narrowing a topic
- marking and assessing

Several decisions should be made prior to leaping head-first into an essay project. Frontline teachers may shake their heads and say, "Yeah, right—in a perfect world, with two educational assistants, a small class load, no supervision, and a prep period every day, I might consider your suggestions." As we strive for excellence—and that's why you're reading this book—consider covering

- distinguishing between formal and informal writing
- using creativity
- narrowing a topic
- marking and assessing the essay (see chapter 3).

Formal vs. Informal Writing

Abrams distinguishes between the formal essay or article and the informal essay this way:

> The formal essay is relatively impersonal: the author writes as an authority, or at least as highly knowledgeable, and expounds the subject in an orderly way. In the informal essay (or "familiar" or "personal essay"), the author assumes a tone of intimacy with his audience, tends to deal with everyday things rather than with public affairs or specialized topics, and writes in a relaxed, self-revelatory, and sometimes whimsical fashion.

To some people, mention alone of the word "essay" suggests formality. However, as teachers today pause to consider their personal attire, the question of formality is seldom suggested. My point? What some consider formal, others do not. In terms of writing an essay, it should be made clear to students where on the continuum of formality the teacher's expectations lie.

My students often had problems trying to grasp the idea of what "formal" means. They frowned when I mentioned "conventions" and grimaced when I tried to explain "agreed-upon standards" or "mutual consent to promote common understanding." I tried to explain using varying degrees of handwriting as an example. I wrote something on the board in my very best cursive handwriting. Then I wrote it in my everyday handwriting, which is a combination of writing and printing. Finally, I printed, as I would if I were quickly jotting down a grocery list. The kids almost got the point.

Perhaps I should have come to class one day in a formal outfit—my "weddings and funerals" attire: suit, shirt and tie, good belt, and polished shoes. I could have gradually become more informal by removing the suit jacket, loosening and later removing the tie. I could have reminded the class what the teaching staff looks like on our Jeans Days. I think the concept may have been clearer.

Understanding the concept of formal versus informal is one thing. Carrying the idea to an essay is the next step. We need to give our students examples of the "suit-to-jeans story" in the context of writing. Here are several:

Formal	Informal
Third-person point of view	May use first-person point of view
Never uses contractions	Contractions aren't a problem
Has a serious, official sound	Can be more like a conversation
More factual	More emotional

Some of the problems students encounter are not so much difficulties with the difference between formal and informal, but result from writing in an overly elementary or clichéd manner. Here are several of my "unfavorites":

- essays that begin with "In this essay…" or "This essay is about…"
- "Well, I'm gonna tell you about…"
- "So he goes, 'Yeah, it's 'cause like, to tell you the truth,…'"
- "Then you know how to solve it & make it better."

On the other hand, few students endeavor to expound and extrapolate beyond both their years and their level of comprehension. Some have been struck down with a serious case of Thesaurusitis. Although, as these students would say, "It is difficult to indoctrinate a superannuated canine with innovative maneuvers," we must try.

In all cases, my only real success has come from using *my* type of exemplars. Sometimes I have used exemplars in the more popular use of the word: an *ideal* example of something, worthy of being copied or imitated. At other times, I have used exemplars with the secondary meaning of the word—a *typical* example.

I have read student work aloud to my class and asked them to raise their hands when they hear what I am looking for—sometimes a good example and sometimes a bad one. If I am looking for "bad" examples, I preface my reading with a short reminder of what I don't like to see in an essay: conversational speech, slang, etc. As I read aloud, students are encouraged to put their hands up if they hear any such examples. The activity involves everyone, underscores what should be avoided in an essay, and uses real examples. I use the same method when I am looking for "good" examples.

Students need to know from the outset which type of essay you are assigning—should it be *formal* or *informal?*

It is the Small Steps philosophy that seems to have the best results. Henry Ford said, "Nothing is particularly hard if you divide it into small jobs."

Teaching Tip
- Never reveal the author of writing that includes "bad" examples. Divulging the name of authors of "good" writing is up to your discretion.

Creativity

After telling your students whether you want a formal essay or an informal one, it would be nice to talk to them about creativity. A popular phrase of the day is "thinking outside the box." My brother tells me that it originates from a puzzle in which one has to join all the dots in a square without lifting the pencil from the page.

.   .   .

.   .   .

.   .   .

Most of us assume that we are constrained by the edges of the square, like being encouraged to color inside the lines, and are thus faced with an impossible task. If we allow our pencil to exceed the boundaries, the task becomes possible. (See Teaching Tip box on page 18 for the solution.)

Although I am a huge fan of creativity, I believe that we need to think both inside and outside the box. If the topic of the day is essays, our students need to both understand the basics *and* be encouraged to be creative.

Teachers and students need a toolbox. In my view, the bigger and more fully equipped the toolbox, the better. We need to show them the tools; they need to use the tools and become adept at employing them to their best advantage. At varying points for different students and to varying degrees, there will come a time when they can get creative.

As I write this, I feel that I sound controlling and totally inside the box. Perhaps an example would help. I often say to my students, "School is school, and life is life. We do things here a certain way because we need to in order to get along. Within the constraints of school, we can have a marvelous, interesting, even exciting (well, almost) time. If we are mindful of the limitations, we can work to push them when necessary to achieve what we need to achieve."

My intention is not to say, "If you always do what you've always done, you'll always get what you always got." I see it as a practical way of dealing with what we face together. If you can understand and appreciate the boundaries, you can then question them and deal with them appropriately.

Can you teach creativity? I'm not sure. You can encourage it, model it, applaud it. Conversely, you can discourage the humdrum, same-old same-old, ticky-tacky cookie-cutter offerings.

Look carefully at the four operations below and react (mentally) to what you see.

$$4 + 3 = 7$$
$$11 - 2 = 9$$
$$6 \times 3 = 17$$
$$15 \div 5 = 3$$

Much of what a Language Arts teacher does lies in the realm of conventions. Our job is to help our kids understand that there are areas where we need to agree to agree, to speak the same "language" so that mutual understanding can be achieved.

Ah yes, essays. The constraints are obvious: paragraph form, a certain level of formality, conventions of grammar, spelling, punctuation, etc., established norms for footnotes, bibliography, and now webography. So where does creativity come in?

Whenever I show this to someone, they say exactly what I said: "There's one wrong." No one has said, "There are three right." My point is that creativity is often viewed as either instinctual or ingrained. We, especially as teachers, unfortunately seem to have the "instinctual" habit of looking for errors. Once we find an error, we can do what we do best; we can teach. We can correct the error!

Probably about half of what I have learned in my life, I have learned from bad examples. I became a teacher, not because of the good teachers I had had in school, but because of the bad ones. I thought, "I could do better than that. Kids deserve more, and I am capable of providing more."

If we want to encourage creativity, we have to understand that we don't totally understand ourselves. I have always seen myself as a "glass half-full" kind of a guy. When I said to myself, "There's one wrong," it came as a bit of a revelation. As I have said, in a perfect world, as we begin an essay project we should discuss creativity with our students. Warn them that they must work within a number of constraints, but do encourage to them to think outside the box whenever it is possible.

Teaching Tip

- Solution to puzzle on page 17:

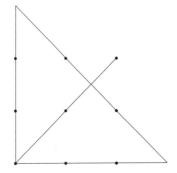

- One way to help students understand creativity is to suggest possible strategies. A favorite of mine is the Opposite View; e.g., rather than assigning the timeworn "How I Spent My Summer Holiday," how about "How I Wish I Had Spent My Summer Holiday"?

Narrowing a Topic

A skill that many of my students lack is the ability to narrow a topic to the point where it is suitable for an essay. I like to give them a little practice, beginning with several straightforward examples. Initially, I write a couple of very general topics—e.g., The Earth, Entertainment—on the board and ask them to be ready to narrow each four times. Together we might come up with gradually narrowed topics like this:

Earth	**Entertainment**
Western Hemisphere	Movies
North America	Comedy
Canada	Animated comedies
Alberta	Disney animated comedies

What I am trying to do is get them to understand that they need to be fairly specific if they are going to write only three body paragraphs.

We continue with the concept of narrowing the given topics four times for a few days. Here are some possible general topics:

Games	Animals	Technology
Sports	Art	Books

The next step is to provide scrambled lists. Here are two examples (for more, see the Narrowing Exercises on pages 20–22):

Put the following lists into order, from general to specific:

Racing	Clothing
Winter sports	People
Downhill skiing	Young people
Skiing	Diapers
Slalom	Babies

For the list above that begins with "Racing," my "correct" order would have been *Winter Sports, Skiing, Downhill skiing, Racing, Slalom*. If the student suggested that she would like to research the three subsets of *famous slalom racers, slalom equipment*, and *how to train for slalom*, I would be a happy camper.

For the list that begins with "Clothing," my general-to-specific order would have been *People, Young people, Babies, Clothing, Diapers*. Again, if a student suggested subsets of *cloth diapers, disposable diapers*, and *environmental impacts*, I would say that all's well that ends well.

Straightforward? Not always. Because I have made up the lists, I have the "correct" order in mind. Experience has shown me that there are other possibilities that are equally correct. A student's explanation of alternatives often proves to be an edifying exercise for all.

For this example, I would be thrilled if some creative student asked to include a paragraph on diapers for senior citizens. Just because the narrowing process included *Babies*, it should not negate the possibility of backtracking to explore an interesting alternative.

Teaching Tips
- The final step to the narrowing process is to try to find at least three subsets for the last and most specific topic. If this can be accomplished, the topic has been sufficiently narrowed to be appropriate for an essay.
- It is helpful to get students to suggest as many as four or five subsets. Once they begin the research process, they may discover that there is not enough information about some of their chosen subsets so having more choices provides flexibility. Sometimes it's okay to have narrow point of view.

Narrowing Exercise #1

Name: _____

Rewrite each of the following lists on the lines provided so that they are in order from **general** to **specific**.

Card games   _____   Blackberry   _____

Games   _____   Hand-held   _____

Texas Hold 'Em   _____   Computers   _____

Poker   _____   Technology   _____

Pie   _____   Writing   _____

Food   _____   Pens   _____

Dessert   _____   Gel   _____

Apple   _____   Communication _____

Clothing   _____   Jokes   _____

Outerwear   _____   Mail   _____

Ski jacket   _____   E-mail   _____

Down-filled   _____   Animated   _____

Pets   _____

Hairball medicine   _____

Methods of giving   _____

Cats   _____

Oral

Narrowing Exercise #2

Name: _____

Rewrite each of the following lists on the lines provided so that they are in order from **general** to **specific**. For the last two groups, add your own ideas of any degree of specificity. e.g. more general, more specific.

Hair loss   _____   Human body   _____

People   _____   Head   _____

Old men   _____   Retina   _____

Comb-overs   _____   Eyes   _____

Men   _____

Furniture   _____   Engraving on lid _____

Hammock   _____   Timepieces   _____

Outdoor   _____   Pocket watch   _____

Summer   _____   Small   _____

Art   _____   Literature   _____

Painting   _____   Novels   _____

Oil   _____   Dramas   _____

             _____   _____

             _____   _____

Narrowing Exercise #3

Name: _____

Rewrite each of the following lists on the lines provided so that they are in order from **general** to **specific**.

Dogs	_____	12-string guitars	_____
Animals	_____	Guitars	_____
Four-legged	_____	String instruments	_____
Retrievers	_____	Tuning	_____
Hunting dog	_____	Music	_____

NBA	_____	Horns	_____
Left guard	_____	Trumpets	_____
Sports	_____	Instrumental	_____
Raptors	_____	Brass	_____
Basketball	_____	Music	_____

Writing	_____	Clothing	_____
Middle schools	_____	Flipflops	_____
Education	_____	Footwear	_____
Public schools	_____	Sandals	_____
Language Arts	_____	Summer	_____
Grade 8	_____		
Essays	_____		

3 Assessment and Marking

If you don't know where you're going, how will you know when you get there?

Chronologically, this step comes near the end of the essay-writing project. However, I have found that explaining the marking/grading/assessing plan is much more helpful to both students and teacher if it is done at the outset.

Before I leap into the practicalities, a few thoughts of a more philosophical nature are important to consider. Students who are concerned about "the mark" are often *overly* concerned about "the mark" and not as concerned as we might wish with how the mark was determined or what it really means. In this new Age of Assessment, of assessing *for* learning as well as assessment *of* learning, teachers are beginning to see some glimmer of hope of not having to give a number, a mark, a quantification for everything. There is more of an appreciation for the journey as well as for the destination.

Semantics also plays a role. The meanings of *marking, grading,* and *assessing* are different for different people. Rick Wormeli notes

> The Latin root of *assessment* is "assidere," meaning "to sit beside." This means that assessment is a coaching, nurturing tool. Its emphasis is not so much on documenting deficiencies as it is on shaping our instructional decisions.... Grades by their very nature are post-learning, and we want students to learn. That means we can't spend a lot of time using grades as learning tools. Instead, we do a lot of formative and specific feedback along the way, regarding what has been accomplished so far.

Most of us would agree.

Marking the Essay

My experience with what I have always called "marking" is that it needs to be visible (not interred in the teacher's mark-book and unearthed or exhumed at report-card time), it needs to be relatively frequent (a Mugwump phrase for "as often as you can possibly can"), and it needs to take into account effort and time on task.

MUGWUMP: a bird who sits on the fence with its mug on one side and its wump on the other. Known to be indecisive. (Well, sort of.)

For me, an essay assignment takes several weeks of class time. Some teachers see this time as a respite from the constant marking that most English teachers do, even if it means facing a mountain of papers at the end. Some teachers appreciate the opportunity to be a facilitator, an encourager, and a coach— and not a policeman. I empathize but I don't agree. There are varying opinions about whether one should mark only the finished product. My tent is pitched in the camp that supports giving part of the student's grade for the work done during the process of creating the product.

The devil is in the details, and we may disagree as to what portion the "getting there" is worth, but I liken the "only mark the finished product" scenario to the Oscars, the film industry's annual award show. Biff Kooldude or Trixie Splendid may end up holding the gold, but they always go on at length about who else should really be up on stage with them. I think it's the same with an essay. If we are really concerned with coaching and nurturing, we need to mark, grade, and assess as many of the steps of the process as we can. Are we doing students a favor by awarding the students who put on a final burst at the end, or who plagiarize, or who get someone else's help? I think not.

Once again, the Small Steps philosophy should come into play. As Madeline Hunter encouraged in *Mastery Teaching*, we must make frequent checks to see that our students stay on track. Time flies when you're having fun, and time flies when students are having too much fun. Days and days can be spent on an essay project and, while you are dancing as fast as you can, there always seems to be a number of students who go quietly about accomplishing very little.

Posting Marks

In order for marks to be visible I had to post the marks for all to see. If I wanted my marking to be relatively frequent, it helped for it to be visible—because if I fell behind in marking and posting results, the more vocal students would always remind me. But posting marks on a class list can be embarrassing; some students are embarrassed by high marks, others by low ones. What to do?

In all of my classes, near the beginning of the year, I would ask the students to decide upon a personal nickname, a nom de plume, an a.k.a., an alias. Several rules applied:

- no names of students in the school (subtle ridicule is a danger)
- no rude names (Ben Dover is one mild example, Mike _____ [I blush at suggesting the surname, so take my word and be on the lookout for this one])
- no names with more than 12 characters (because they won't fit in our electronic grading system)

Without going into laborious detail, I would post my marks, using an electronic marking system that allowed me to substitute the student identification number with the student nickname. As long as I posted the names in a different order from the known-to-many order of the class list, each student's identity remained a secret. Many chose to share their nicknames—but that often turned into a lesson in life for them, and I was always kind enough to allow them to submit a new moniker if they ran into trouble sharing their original one with a poor secret keeper. The results were effective. Each time I posted the mark updates, considerable interest was created and any errors I had made were quickly brought to my attention. In summary, the posting process helped keep me on track and on time with my marking, the students knew what they had done and how well, and there were never any surprises at report-card time.

Before students begin their essay project, it is only fair to explain how the marking will be done.

Marking needs to
- be visible
- be relatively frequent
- assess effort and time on task

Sample List of Class Nicknames
Heidi
TOPDOG
Shorty
Dread
boarderkid!
Blondy
Schmeeb
~sugar~
Duff
Red Skull
Tigger
Choco Toco

Assessing Effort and Time on Task

Assessing effort and time on task became a lot easier after I had taught Physical Education and Drama. In those two subjects, I established the habit of taking a few minutes at the end of each class to assign an "effort and involvement" mark to every student.

At first it was difficult, but it got easier and easier. I regularly posted the marks and was rewarded for it. Those who did well were pleased to see that I acknowledged their participation; those who did not do well often acknowledged aloud, as they read the list, their understanding of their shortcomings.

My mother used to say, "Take turns with the things you neglect." I must admit that I took turns not marking students daily for effort and participation. But when I did, it really worked.

Teaching Tip
- When marking daily effort and involvement, use a class list and assign each student a mark out of 10.

Checking Along the Way

With specific reference to essay writing, I would suggest a variety of checks along the way. Accomplishing all of these suggestions would make you a candidate for Teacher of the Century—choose what works for you.

Things the Student Can Check

When a student is doing an essay unit, the most helpful self-monitoring is done through self-reflection on a journal page set aside for the purpose of evaluating progress during the writing stage. On predetermined dates, or at certain stages of the journey (e.g. at the end of every class), ask students to comment on

- What is going well
- Where I am having problems
- What I need to do next
- What I accomplished today (or since last time)

This journal page serves several purposes: it forces students to evaluate themselves as they proceed, it is motivational, it helps the teacher know how best to help the student, and it allows for planning and goal setting.

There are
- things the student can check
- things that classmates can check
- things that parents can check
- things the teacher can check

When it comes to revision, the student-author can check his or her own ideas to see if they are up to COAD (see page 75), or use a Legend and Color system (see page 76).

Teaching Tip
- Rather than having students keep the accumulation of journal pages in their normal journal (a duotang filled with looseleaf paper and stored at the back of the class), have them keep them in the binder with the other essay work. Once the essay is finished, the pages can be placed in the student's journal.

Things That Classmates Can Check

Let me clarify a potential problem before you read further. Students in my classes are told at the beginning of the school year, and then are reminded as often as it seems necessary, that whatever they write may have three possible audiences: the teacher, their parents, their peers. At no time should they write anything not suitable to be shared.

Day in and day out, a climate of trust has to be established. With some classes it's easier than with others, but students must be shown that you, the teacher, are the champion of fair play, someone who gets respect by showing respect and who administers justice to those who bully.

During the editing stage, classmates play a vital role in the Mackenzie Snake (see page 83). In another version of the editing process recommended by high-school teacher Lisa Robertson, classmates use pencil crayons, color coding, underlining, and circling to assess one another's work (see page 76).

Yet another aid in the task of overcoming students' fears about sharing their work with peers is the whole concept of "code names." As explained on page 24, a paper with a code name on it is not impossible to attribute to a given student, but it makes the task just a bit harder.

Things That Parents Can Check

My grandmother used to say, "Many hands make light work." (I used to think she was saying, "Many hands make like work.") As teachers, we know how important parents are, but often fail to involve them during the journey. I have always felt that I was missing an opportunity to get some needed assistance.

At parent–student–teacher conferences, parents would often say to me, "Every night at supper, I ask _____how school's going, and I always get the same response, 'Oh fine.'" My suggestion has always been to be more specific —and somewhat dogged. I encourage parents to try asking about a particular subject, or about an assignment or project that they know about. I warn them not to accept general responses, to look for specifics.

While teaching essay writing, I find that getting parents to initial and date things is helpful. If the essay topic is assigned, get the parent to initial and date the assignment page. If the essay allows for some choice, get the parent to initial and date the choice that the student makes. Choose subsections of the essay for more initialing and dating: the outline, the introductory and/or concluding paragraph, a section of rough notes, the rough copy after the Mackenzie Snake (page 83), the good copy before it's handed in, the good copy after it has been marked.

Experience has shown me that some parents do not want to be involved, won't initial a work in progress, and even accuse teachers of getting parents to do the teachers' work for them. Experience has also shown that this type of parent causes some of us to stop doing what we know is helpful to many—and needs to be done. Hang in there.

Things the Teacher Can Check

In a 53-minute (or whatever odd number your school has) class with a room of twenty-something or even thirty-something students, after the announcements and administrivia, and following some type of teaching to the group, there is less than a minute per day to spend with each child. So what can you possibly accomplish one-on-one?

Often my best tools were a class list and a clipboard. With class list in hand, I found that I could keep track of who was doing what and had done what, who had chosen what topic, and who was supposed to be working with whom. By using the class list on a clipboard, I was able to check a wide variety of things. Some ended up being for my own awareness, and some ended up on the actual "marked for a grade" lists that became part of the overall mark.

Because essay writing is primarily an individual activity, I spent most of my time on cruise patrol. I offered suggestions, made constructive criticisms, assisted in helping students help themselves. Most importantly, the teacher needs to check with everyone. We know that it is virtually impossible to check with everyone, every day. With my class list, I could see with whom I had met and who remained.

Teaching Tips
- At least twice a year (in September and again at midyear, perhaps) use the class list to create pairs and threesomes of students so that you can easily form groups. If you need larger groups, it is easy to combine existing pairs and triads into foursomes or sixsomes.
- Try not to give in to the temptation to give answers during one-on-one time.

In preparing this book, I met with many teachers to see what they thought a book on teaching the essay should contain. I also asked them to share things that have worked particularly well for them. Penny Crawford-Ritz, a high-school English teacher, is a big fan of the beginning-of-the-class mini-lesson. Her experience has taught her that short, immediately pertinent lessons are helpful to her students. One of the things that she can then check as a teacher is that a particular lesson is being put to proper use.

Using Assessment Tools

At the end of the day, when all is said and done, and when the smoke clears, I have always appreciated specifics. Exactly what can the teacher mark, and how can he or she mark it?

Rubrics

Many teachers today prefer the simplicity and speed of a rubric. Although I am not a big fan of this type of marking, I appreciate the speed part of the equation, and have learned a few ideas about how the rubric can be helpful to students.

Sue Merry, a high-school English teacher, looks at a rubric entry in "Supporting Evidence":

Support is explicit, precise, and deliberately chosen to reinforce the student's ideas in an effective judicious way. A strong connection to the student's ideas is maintained.

Sue gives the student top marks in this category but wants to be a bit more specific:

<u>Support</u> is explicit, precise, and <u>deliberately chosen to reinforce the student's ideas</u> in an effective judicious way. A strong connection to the student's ideas is maintained.

Well worth noting is a resource that has recently come to my attention. It is a series of three small books by Kathleen Gregory, Caren Cameron, and Anne Davies titled *Setting and Using Criteria*, *Self-Assessment and Goal-Setting*, and *Conferencing and Reporting*.

Sue uses a highlighter on each student's rubric marking sheet to note specific bits of information. For this black and white publication, I have substituted underlining for highlighting.

The student knows that he scored 5/5, and he also knows that his teacher felt that the deliberate choice of supportive information was a highlight.

When Sue considered the same student's essay in the "Matters of Correctness" area, she assigned a mark of 4/5 and highlighted one concept:

> This writing demonstrates competence in control of correct sentence construction, usage, grammar, and mechanics. Minor errors in complex language structures are understandable considering the circumstances.

The student can see that he did not score perfectly in this category, but has been told that his proper use of grammar stands out as being worthy of mention.

Having confessed that I am not a fan of rubrics, let me take a quick look at what one of the "Pros from Dover" has to say about them. Alfie Kohn, educator and author, states, "As long as the rubric is only one of several sources, as long as it doesn't drive the instruction, it could conceivably play a constructive role." Taken out of context, one might assume that Mr. Kohn is on-side with rubrics. Hardly. Earlier in the article he writes

> The ultimate goal of authentic assessment must be the elimination of grades. But rubrics actually help to *legitimate* grades by offering a new way to derive them. They do nothing to address the terrible reality of students who have been led to focus on getting A's rather than on making sense of ideas.

Having been a teacher for over 30 years, I have seen the call for "the elimination of grades" numerous times. It never happened. Perhaps I shouldn't have, but I resigned myself to working within the system as it existed and did my best to deal with the imperfect but ever-present method of reporting student progress —grades.

Marking Keys

My personal preference in the field of marking, grading, and assessing, is a numeric scale. Quite often, I would use a 10-point scale. Subconsciously, many people convert a mark out of 10 to a percentage. If I give a 5/10, I see a 50% result. In my books, 50% is a pass—but just. An 8/10 or 80% is an honors mark and denotes a significant accomplishment.

Another favorite was the "a mark for each thing I am looking for" scale. If I asked for a minimum of four supporting details, I might assign 4 marks. If I asked that the student include at least three examples of figurative speech, there would be a space for it on the marking key:

Figurative Language   /3

In instances where I had to judge quality rather than simply check that the required information was included, I usually favored a scale of 3:

1 it's there, but only just
2 a satisfactory offering
3 a quality example

If "four supporting details" were required, the marking key would likely show a mark out of 12; i.e., four supporting details each allotted a mark out of three.

Creating a marking key (see pages 30–31) requires considerable work, and it has both advantages and disadvantages. In my experience, I found that a key that had room for both numeric judgments as well as room for comments was the best. Numbers alone can be too restrictive. It is said that figures can lie and liars can figure, but, as already stated, we live in a world of numbers. My suggestion is this: decide what is most important in the assignment at hand, break it down into manageable parts, and assign each section a numeric value—and then get on with teaching kids. In the words of Yogi Berra, "Baseball is 90% mental, the other half is physical."

A Final Word on Marking

Knowing how to mark effectively, what to mark for, and how to share the marks with students so that the marks are helpful are all important aspects of the whole marking, grading, assessing game. A critical element is getting the marking done in a timely fashion.

It cannot be quantified, but *timely praise* is one of the most important and memorable methods of assessment. Not an official or widely acknowledged "Pro from Dover," but a colleague, Lucille Gleddie, taught me about the power of *timely praise*. Lucille took the initiative and the time, usually a matter of seconds, to put her praise into words, and she did so right after the praiseworthy act had been committed. I ask you, dear reader, to look back on your entire life, and try to remember the number of times that someone has praised you. As we consider the specific topic of essay writing, and the bigger picture (teaching), and the biggest picture (our lives), think of how *timely praise* can be shared to let others know how we grade, mark, or assess an act, an action, or an activity.

Teaching Tips
- Hand out marking keys at the beginning of the project.
- When creating a marking key, consider including both positive and negative aspects of written work; e.g. Positive: Effective Supporting Detail, Smooth Flow, Interesting Ideas; Negative: Run-on sentences, Spelling Errors, Neatness. When marking a student's paper, simply circle the appropriate aspect.
- Realize that the due date does not have to be the same for one and all. If essays are due during the week of, say April 24–28, you will not find yourself having to mark a whole class's essays overnight. Class time during that week should not be given to essay work, but students have the time at home or at school to complete their essays.

Essay Marking Key

Name_____

marked by ❑ author ❑ peer ❑ parent/guardian ❑ teacher

Title ❑ tells/suggests the topic ❑ captures interest /3

Introductory paragraph

Thesis Statement Alone   Personal Comment or Anecdote

Questions   Opposite View   Quotation   Startling Statement   Mix

❑ prepares the reader for what is to follow

❑ identifies order of sub-topics

❑ arouses interest /10

Body paragraph #1

Topic sentence: beginning   middle   end

Development: Facts & Statistics   Reasons   Examples   Quotes

Opinions   Experiences   Senses

Order: Time   Importance   Most to Least Obvious

Known to New   Simple to Complex   Other

Information: ❑ Sufficient ❑ Ideas are related ❑ Smooth flow

❑ Effective transitions /10

Body paragraph #2

Topic sentence: beginning   middle   end

Development: Facts & Statistics   Reasons   Examples   Quotes

Opinions   Experiences   Senses

Order: Time   Importance   Most to Least Obvious

Known to New   Simple to Complex   Other

Information: ❑ Sufficient ❑ Ideas are related ❑ Smooth flow

❑ Effective transitions /10

Body paragraph #3

Topic sentence: beginning   middle   end

Development: Facts & Statistics   Reasons   Examples   Quotes

Opinions   Experiences   Senses

Order: Time   Importance   Most to Least Obvious

Known to New   Simple to Complex   Other

Information: ❑ Sufficient ❑ Ideas are related ❑ Smooth flow

❑ Effective transitions /10

Essay Marking Key (cont'd)

Concluding paragraph

❑ Begins with a transitional device   ❑ Does not but is still worded effectively

Restates the Main Points   The Future, Suggestions for Action

Questions   Personal Comment or Anecdote   Cyclic Return

❑ Brings the essay to a smooth conclusion   /10

Spelling	❑ some errors but possibly because you have been a risk taker!	
	❑ more care required	/3
Capitalization	❑ you have capitalized words that should not be capitalized	
	❑ you have not capitalized words that should be capitalized	/3
Punctuation	. ? ! , ; : " "	
	' contractions ' ownership	/3
Sentences	fragments run-on varied styles varied lengths	
	other _____	/3
Grammar & Usage	❑ consistent verb tense ❑ no abbreviations	
	❑ avoided slang ❑ subject-verb agreement	/3
Areas of strength	Areas to work on	

_____ %   /68

4 Before Writing Begins

Plan your work, and work your plan.

One year—when things were particularly hectic, and it was spring and time was running out, and it was essay time—I had my students do every single part of the essay project except writing out the good copy. Many were aghast. Since that fateful year I have, in fact, been able to sleep nights knowing that the lion's share of the work had been done. Sometimes you just have to decide where it is wisest to spend your time.

Students who are often unwilling to get down to work seem to fall under some Spell of Reversal when it's essay time. I have found that I can't get them to slow down, to plan first and work second. I wish it were a case of "Rarin' to go, but can't go for rarin'"—but it isn't. I appreciate the enthusiasm of youth, but far too many short stories from earlier in the term show that the initial enthusiasm of mentioning every detail soon fades to abrupt endings, like the infamous, "And then he woke up. It had all been a dream."

We often hear that our unstructured youth really do want structure. Well, here's a golden opportunity to provide some. When I truly performed my role as teacher-facilitator-leader, and wasn't busy running after the others ("for I am their leader"), I was able to show my students how to proceed step-by-step in an orderly and productive way.

Planning the Essay

When I first do essays with a Grade 8 class, most of the students are beginning at square one. That is not to say that they haven't been "taught essays" before; however, what they have retained seems minimal.

The steps in planning an essay are
1. Brainstorming
2. Creating and organizing scattergrams
3. Developing an outline

1. Brainstorming

I first ask for ideas, topics of interest, something that kids in general but these students in particular would like to find out more about. We brainstorm. I used to launch right into the You-call-out-the-ideas-and-I'll-write-on-the-board routine. I still do that, but I give them three or four minutes to talk among themselves to get the juices flowing.

When the three or four minutes were up, the students would call out suggestions; I would write them on the board. I would sometimes ask permission to reword a suggestion, or piggyback an idea of my own onto one of theirs. In the end we had lots of ideas.

2. Scattergrams

The next step is to create a scattergram. I do not know where this idea came from, but it has worked wonders for me. In essence, a student is asked to

1. write the topic in the middle of the page
2. cover the page with every conceivable idea, thought, aspect of the topic, or possibility that comes to mind.
3. use a system of colors or symbols to group/categorize the ideas
4. create a legend that names each group
5. number the main groups in the legend in a logical order
6. number the ideas within each group in a logical order
7. create an outline based on the organization of the scattergram

It has often been my habit to work along with the class and create my own version of whatever it was I assigned to them. Having students mimic the teacher's version will always be a problem but is not insurmountable.

Here's a sample of a scattergram I did on Golf.

superstitions ball markers becoming a pro

sponsor's exemptions Canadian Tour PGA

size of marker Nationwide Tour Q school caddies

dealing with pressure expenses quality of life

game vs. business local – regional – national – international

equipment **GOLF** amateur vs. pro

marks on the golf ball signed autographs scoreboard

playing one hole at a time other idiosyncrasies

As you can see, I wrote my topic—GOLF—in the middle of the page. My next step was to scatter ideas all over the page, as I considered some of the things about golf that intrigue me.

My next step was to group similar ideas. I chose to underline some, circle some, and put rectangles around some: all the underlined items had something to do with habits or superstitions that professional golfers have; the circled items have something to do with becoming a professional golfer; I put rectangles around the pressures that pro golfers face.

Because my students could not see my mental process, I created a legend.

_____ Habits and Superstitions

Becoming a Professional Golfer

Pressures

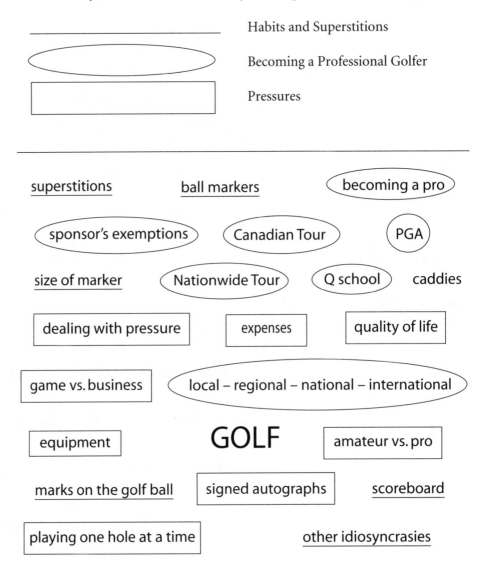

Having put my ideas into major categories, I discuss with my class how to order these big ideas. In this instance, we determine that we should first talk about how to become a professional golfer, then to discuss what pressures the pros face, and conclude with some of the interesting superstitions.

The next step is to plan a logical order within each of these subsections. Using superscript numbers, I suggest a possible sequence for the underlined items.

- I might order them in a ground-up arrangement; i.e., the topic—superstitions—followed by ball markers, size of marker, marks on the golf ball, scoreboard (some players think it's unlucky to watch the scoreboard), and finally other idiosyncrasies.
- For the circled items, I number the ideas and then ask the class to figure out why I had chosen that order.
- For the third category, the ideas in rectangles, we discuss possibilities and then order the ideas accordingly.

Teaching Tips
- When categorizing ideas in a scattergram, it is quite normal to have an idea—or a few— left over, not fitting into any of the categories.
- Once major categories have been determined, paragraph numbers can be added to the legend.
- Another option for numbering the ideas in the subsections is to have groups of students meet and plan an order, then share it with the class.

For the sake of practice, I have included another scattergram that I originally used for a character description. I invented a character, JoJo McCool, then listed both physical and personality characteristics. The samples that follow show the progression from bare-naked scattergram to one that has been categorized to one that has been ordered with superscripts.

baggy jeans   likes to tell jokes

friendly   frizzy hair
              designer running shoes

flowered shirt   Jo Jo McCool   gold
                                                      ring in nose

parts hair
in middle   brilliant white teeth

                                                      faded
                              mirrored sunglasses   blue jeans

always willing to share

                              shoes are worn out

brownish-blonde hair

                              nice to new students

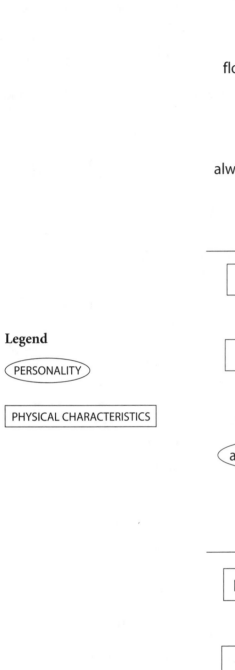

Legend

PERSONALITY

PHYSICAL CHARACTERISTICS

3. Outline

I try to show the students that planning and essay can be done quickly, and that it is not a make-work project. It takes a little convincing to get them to do the final step—creating an outline from their scattergrams—but I have a plan. I get a student to time me as I write out an outline based on the numbering we have done. Each time I do this, I prove that planning is a necessary, but not necessarily time-consuming, assignment. I stress "planning your work, and working your plan."

Doing the outline also helps reinforce the bigger picture of the entire outline of the essay. The Golf outline looked like this:

Title—to be determined

I. Introductory Paragraph

II. Becoming a professional golfer
    A. Local – Regional – National – International
    B. Q school
    C. Canadian tour
    D. Nationwide tour
    E. PGA
    F. Sponsor's exemptions

III. Pressures on a professional golfer
    A. Game vs. Business
    B. Amateur vs. Pro
    C. Expenses
    D. Quality of Life
    E. Other pressures
        1. Equipment
        2. Playing one hole at a time
        3. Signing autographs

IV. Superstitions and Habits
    A. Ball markers and size of marker
    B. Marks on the golf ball
    C. Scoreboard reading
    D. Other idiosyncrasies

V. Concluding Paragraph

I try to teach my students the format of outlines by simply using them in as many different settings as possible. When I give a set of notes in our Poetry Unit, they look like this:

I. Sound Effects
   A. Rhyme
      1. End
      2. Internal
      3. Near
   B. Rhythm
      1. Stressed syllables
      2. Unstressed syllables
   C. Euphony
      1. Alliteration
      2. Onomatopoeia
      3. Pun

II. Thought or Emotional Effects
   A. Figurative Language
      1. Simile
      2. Metaphor
   B. Compressed Thought
      1. Hyperbole
      2. Personification

Journal writing is daily in the fall, but is done only twice a week later in the school year.

When we do our journal writing, the front board or overhead would show something like this:

Today's topics:
I. An embarrassing moment
   A. For you
   B. For someone you know
II. What little kids should know
   A. Right now
   B. When they get older
III. Your choice

By repeating the Number – Letter – Number sequence used in outlining, the students learn it almost by osmosis. When it comes times for official essay writing, a few added details are required.

My students never got the concept of needing at least two sub-ideas in a swooning moment of "Aha!" Several exercises (especially Outlines #1 and #2 in the Outlining Exercise on page 39) as well as several reminders seemed to help. Outline #3 in the Outlining Exercise on page 40 is an example of an outlining disaster. See Corrected Outlines on page 41 to check student work.

Outlining Exercise

Correct the following outlines after discussing each with a classmate.

Outline #1: What is Poetry?

I.   Sound Effects

    A. Rhyme
        4. End
        5. Internal
        6. Near
    B. Rhythm
        3. Stressed syllables
    C. Euphony
        4. Alliteration
        5. Onomatopoeia
        6. Pun

II. Thought or Emotional Effects

    A. Figurative Language
        3. Simile
    B. Compressed Thought
        3. Hyperbole

Outline #2: Journal Writing

1. My thoughts about Grade ____ so far:

    a. The students in my homeroom
    B. New teachers
    3. Subjects compared to last year
    d. Other differences

II. A dream

    A. One I had recently (or keep having)
3. Your Choice

Outlining Exercise (cont'd)

Outline #3: Short Story Plot

I. Introduction

    1. Setting
        a. Time
        B. Place
        c. Mood
    B. Introduction of main characters
        1. Round and flat characters

2. Initial Incident

    i. Main conflict
    ii. Man vs. Man, Man vs. Himself, Man vs. Nature

III. Rising Action

    A. A series of events that build suspense
    4. Climax
    5. Epilogue or Resolution
        a. Loose ends are tied up
        b. Often brief if it exists at all

Corrected Outlines

Outline #1: What is Poetry?

I. Sound Effects

    A. Rhyme
        1. End
        2. Internal
        3. Near
    B. Rhythm — stressed syllables
    C. Euphony
        1. Alliteration
        2. Onomatopoeia
        3. Pun

II. Thought or Emotional Effects

    A. Figurative Language — simile
    B. Compressed Thought — hyperbole

Outline #2: Journal Writing

I. My thoughts about Grade ___ so far:

    A. The students in my homeroom
    B. New teachers
    C. Subjects compared to last year
    D. Other differences

II. A dream — one I had recently
(or keep having)

III. Your Choice

Outline #3: Short Story Plot

I. Introduction

    A. Setting
        1. Time
        2. Place
        3. Mood
    B. Introduction of main characters — round and flat characters

II. Initial Incident

    A. Main conflict
    B. Man vs. Man, Man vs. Himself, Man vs. Nature

III. Rising Action — a series of events that build suspense

IV. Climax

V. Epilogue or Resolution

    A. Loose ends are tied up
    B. Often brief if it exists at all

Because some outlines are quite specific, I have shown students that they can sub-divide up to five times. Following the Number – Letter – Number system, it looks like this:

    I.
        A.
            1.
                a.
                    i.

There's always someone who asks, "Yeah, well, what if the *i* has a couple of subsets?" My response has been, "Yeah, well, that's not very likely." A short pause for effect is followed by the explanation that two more subsets do exist: parentheses around the lower-case letter (a) and the lower-case Roman numeral (i). After that, as Ogden Nash would say, "And I will bet a silk pajama" that there are no more subsets than that.

From Scattergram to Outline

For those who need it, here is an example of the whole process of planning:

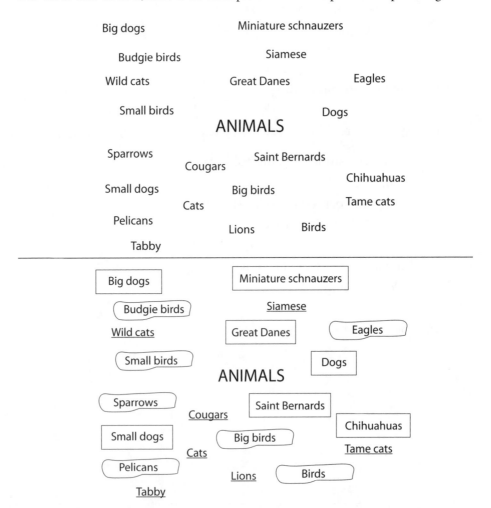

Animals

I.   Dogs
    A. Big dogs
       1. Great Danes
       2. Saint Bernards
    B. Small dogs
       1. Miniature Schnauzers
       2. Chihuahuas

II. Cats
    A. Tame cats
       1. Siamese
       2. Tabby
    B. Wild cats
       1. Cougars
       2. Lions

III. Birds
    A. Big birds
       1. Eagles
       2. Pelicans
    B. Small birds
       1. Sparrows
       2. Budgie birds

Teaching Tips

- Point out that minor changes occur as an outline is created from a scattergram.
- The first outline should be considered a work in progress. Once the research begins, more changes may occur.
- Emphasize the fact that each idea must have two sub-ideas, or it must stand alone. For example, in "What Is Poetry?" on page 38, there are three sub-ideas under the idea of *Rhyme*; if there was only the sub-idea *End*, it would appear on the same line as *Rhyme*.
- Use the Outline Template on page 44 to get students started on their own outlines.

Gathering Information

A student writing a research essay or a critical response essay needs to find information that will support the thesis, ideas that explain the student's point of view. There are many sources of information that a student can easily access.

Sources of Information

People

One of the best, and often easiest to access, sources of information is a real, live human being. Like hiding in plain sight, the most obvious things are not always

Outline Template

Name _____

I. _____

    A. _____

       1. _____

       2. _____

    B. _____

       1. _____

       2. _____

II. _____

    A. _____

       1. _____

       2. _____

    B. _____

       1. _____

       2. _____

III. _____

    A. _____

       1. _____

       2. _____

    B. _____

       1. _____

       2. _____

so obvious. The most overlooked "real live person" a student can use as a resource is her/himself. As teachers, we can begin by getting our students to jot down what they already know about a topic before they start looking farther afield.

Someone in the school, at home, or in the community is likely to have more than enough knowledge about a chosen topic. My parents used to say, "They sure like to talk about their horses, don't they!" They meant that, in many instances, people like to talk about what *they* are interested in and what *they* are doing. In essay research, this can be used to advantage. If a student can find someone who knows about a topic, the chances are pretty good that they will be more than willing to tell the essay writer all about it.

Knowing that "people" are one of your best resources is one thing. Accessing this untapped resource is something else. For me, the key to making this work was nothing more than finding the will (and the time) to make it work. On one occasion, my class was studying local history. I sat down and thought of every senior citizen I knew who had lived in our town long enough to be able to share some of its history. It didn't take long. I called them, set up a date at the local seniors' centre, bussed my class down there, and then did a merry-go-round-the-tables discussion. Small groups of students listened to and interacted with one senior at a time. With one minor exception, it was a huge success. The exception came when one of my Grade 9 girls accepted a chaw of chewing tobacco and found it not to her liking.

In the Possible Sources of Information flow chart on page 46, I have categorized the People resources into three groups: Me, People I Know, and People Who Know People I Know. I offer myself to my classes as one of the People I Know. I further offer people who I know as sources of information. In one class, a boy was researching golf; I know the golf pro at a local course. Another boy was researching how recreation might be seen as an alternative to involvement in delinquent behavior; I know a policeman. A girl was interested in housing for the impoverished; I know the mayor, who had been involved in housing projects for low-income citizens. In each instance, I offered to connect the student with the local expert. I even phoned the experts to be sure that they could help. In each instance, the students chose not to take advantage of the opportunity. Why? My bet is that they lacked the self-confidence to make a phone call to a stranger. I know that I would have been too frightened to call a stranger when I was in Grade 8.

Once, one of my students wanted to know more about the game of pool. I phoned a poolhall owner while the student stood beside me. We played a little bit of "he asked–he said" telephone relay as questions were posed and answers were given through me, but it did work.

Print Sources

Any "print source" can be useful. Despite the fact that students would prefer to surf the Web, the bottom line is getting the goods on the topic in question. All the librarians with whom I have had the privilege of working have provided my classes with a variety of excellent books.

For general information, the oft-overlooked encyclopedia can be an excellent source. The old-fashioned bound editions or an online encyclopedia offer plenty of data—especially when we are looking for the amount of detail appropriate to the construction of a three-paragraph body. Quite often the library will have excellent books on a topic that does not require the latest, up-to-date information. Some libraries will have periodicals (magazines) and even newspapers that

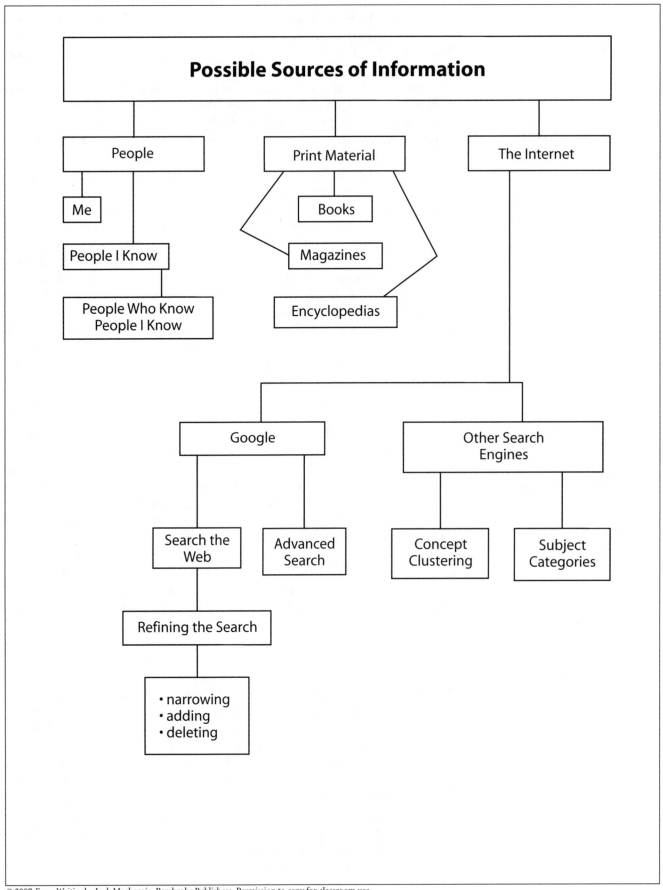

Possible Sources of Information

- People
  - Me
  - People I Know
    - People Who Know People I Know
- Print Material
  - Books
  - Magazines
  - Encyclopedias
- The Internet
  - Google
    - Search the Web
      - Refining the Search
        - narrowing
        - adding
        - deleting
    - Advanced Search
  - Other Search Engines
    - Concept Clustering
    - Subject Categories

In my experience, students' inability to find information in a print source stems from
- not knowing *how* to find the information
- not knowing precisely *what* it is they are looking for

We learned that if you could look it up in the phone book, then you could look it up in almost any book.

can be useful—especially for late-breaking news. The rub? Students often lack the ability to find the information.

How: Learning how to find information in a book can be both a prerequisite step to essay writing and a part of the essay-writing project. Because the students have varied topics, a generic beginning was always helpful for me.

1. Use a class set of telephone books. Easy to acquire and suitable for many years, the phone book allowed me to challenge all students to find the same information—often in the form of a race. I could teach about

- guide words: then see how long it takes to find the page that shows Thelma Smith's phone number.
- the table of contents: then look at major sections in the phone book that many do not know even existed
- the index to the yellow pages: then discuss major sections and subsections, and synonyms (e.g., if I wanted a haircut, did I look under Barbers, Beauty Salons, Hair Stylists?)
- skimming for information (words in bold face, the use of color)

2. Use a class set of Social Studies or Science texts. Many of the same skills can be studied—using a table of contents, using an index, skimming—but the texts have the added advantage of introductions and conclusions to chapters (an excellent source for an overview), topic sentences, pictures, diagrams and charts, and summary questions.

What: A critical part of planning their work is that students must know as specifically as possible what it is they are looking for. I encourage my students to pose questions and then to search for answers. Frequently, getting answers to some of the 5W's and H is a start. Suppose a student wants to write about an issue that affects teens: scholarships. Whether by creating a scattergram or web, or some other method, they will come up with questions such as

What scholarships are available?	When is the application deadline?
Who can apply?	Who has the detailed information?
Are there any strings attached?	How does the money have to be spent?

If students have specific questions, they can look for specific answers. If the questions are seen as puzzle pieces and the answers provide clues as to how to arrange the pieces, it becomes clearer throughout the research process that the puzzle can be pieced together successfully.

The Internet

When students are using the Internet to research, the best advice that I can give is to be specific, and to use the advanced search capabilities of the computer.

Many students seem to be able to use the Internet to find the information that they require for their essays. Many do not. Those who do not tend to spend lots of time looking but very little time finding. They don't seem to mind, but class time gets eaten up and the payback is small.

Being specific: Students benefit from having either narrowed the topic (see Narrowing Exercises on pages 20–22) that they list in their search, or from having specific questions in mind for which they need answers.

One of my students was writing an essay assigned to be on a personal issue—teenagers being discriminated against. Someone had told her that discrimination based on a person's age was known as "ageism." She loved the new word and did an Internet search on it. In less than two seconds she received a list of 873,000 sites. What did she do? She did what most of my students do. She started skimming the first page looking for a site that looked promising, and then the second, and so on. It did not occur to her that many of the sites dealt with discrimination against older people, or that many of the sites dealt with all types of ageism. A good teacher might suggest that she try to be more specific. When she typed in *ageism* and *adolescence*, she got 69,800 responses. When she typed in, using quotation marks, *"ageism"* and *"adolescence"* she got 39,900 responses. The last number is about 5% of the first list of responses. Could my young lady read or even browse almost 40,000 sites? No. But it seems to make sense to cut out as much deadwood and cut off as many dead-end streets as possible.

Searching the Net should be a "work in progress" and not a static endeavor. As a student sees results that are *not* what is wanted, he or she can refine or narrow the search.

Using advanced search capabilities: My students were impressed to note that an advanced search allows you to look for information in a particular file format. One boy searched for only PowerPoint presentations. Another, who was researching the samurai, discovered that many of the sites were about a popular video game—not what he wanted, as his research was on the historical Japanese samurai. He was thrilled to discover that he could limit his search by telling the computer what NOT to include—no video games.

Teaching Tips

- When recommending that students look to themselves as sources of information, be careful. I have assigned a research essay, only to have some students write only what they already know. In instances such as this, the student doesn't do any research, doesn't learn anything about the process of researching—and certainly doesn't learn anything new about a topic they are obviously interested in.
- Work with your students to find a way to make them more comfortable with contacting and getting information from adults they do not know.
- Remind your students that, when they are looking for information, any librarian can be a great asset.
- As always, when teaching How to Use Print Sources (page 47) the trick is to achieve the carry-over from looking for information as a large group in a contest-type setting to looking for information when students are on their own.
- At the beginning level, magazines and newspapers do not often play a significant role in essay research. Mention their usefulness, but don't be surprised to find that they will be used only by students who subscribe to a magazine or who stumble on information in a newspaper "accidentally."

Making Notes

Finding one or more sources of information is a beginning. The next critical step is to make notes that can be used in writing the essay. In my experience, point-form notes are the best kind:

- The essence can be gleaned from a source without having to worry about plagiarism.
- Point-form notes don't take a lot of time.
- When you gather information from various sources, it is easy to see what information is redundant.

Many teachers will likely find the Notes template on page 50 too small. It is important to keep in mind the needs of *your* students, and to reformat the form if necessary.

See the Notes template on page 50; it consists mainly of lines on which to note ideas, and is divided into four sections: Points for Main Idea #1, #2, and #3, plus room for "Other Points." The key to using the Notes Template is to have a clear commitment to the three main ideas. As information is found, it can be written in the appropriate place.

How can we get students to assess the information they acquire? When we stress that some sources of information are reliable and some are not, we remind them that just because something is written down doesn't make it true. Once again, some of the 5W's can be brought into play. Have students ask themselves

Alternatives to point-form notes include highlighting text (on hard copy or electronically) and writing summaries of good sources of relevant information.

- WHO wrote it? (Is that person knowledgeable?)
- WHAT bias might that person bring to the topic?
- WHEN was it written? (the more up-to-date the better)
- WHERE did I find the information? (Is the source reliable?)

Quoting and Citing Sources

Whatever method is employed to take notes, it is possible and, sadly, even likely that the problem of plagiarism will arise. Hopefully, forewarned is forearmed. In my classes, I state simply the following:

Plagiarism, the use of the exact words taken from a resource without clearly quoting or acknowledging that source, is cheating. It is like passing off someone else's work as your own. To plagiarize is a major offence.

I make it as easy as possible for students to cite their sources, and therefore have considerable success in avoiding plagiarism. Admittedly, the bibliographical details would have both the MLA and the APA people frowning, but my students are just beginners.

1. I ask my students to note the author, title, publisher, and date of publication of books that they use.

Author's last name, Author's first name <u>Title.</u> Name of publisher, Date of publication.
Mackenzie, John <u>How to Succeed in Life</u>. Goodguy Books, 2001

Notes

Essay topic: _____ Name _____

MAIN IDEA #1 _____

POINTS

_____

_____

_____

_____

MAIN IDEA #2 _____

POINTS

_____

_____

_____

_____

MAIN IDEA #3 _____

POINTS

_____

_____

_____

_____

OTHER POINTS

_____

_____

_____

_____

2. For magazines, page numbers are required.

Author's last name, Author's first name "Title of article" <u>Periodical name</u>, periodical date, page numbers
Bo Peep, Little "Counting Sheep to Get to Sleep" <u>Country Digest</u>, Spring 2006, 33–37

I always ask my students to jot down source notes on information as they gather it.

3. For information from the Internet, I ask only that they note the URL and the title (if clear) of the site they accessed.
4. I ask that the bibliographies appear as endnotes. To try to footnote on the same page seems too difficult.

Teaching Tips

• Cover point-form notes throughout the school year, as you teach about main and supporting ideas, as you underline the key words and phrases in exam questions, as you discuss padding and verbosity. The students may not get the concept of point form right away, and may work harder than smarter, but it will come with time and practice and guidance.

• If it is possible for the student to have consistent access to a school computer or (and this never worked for me) to have an ongoing connection between a school computer and the one at home, an electronic version of the Notes templates (page 50) is possible. The electronic version offers the advantage (perhaps a dubious one) of allowing the cutting and pasting of information.

• Because there are so many small steps along the way (at least in the sequence that I employ), it was almost impossible for a student to plagiarize large portions of an essay. However, if you say, "Go at it and I will mark the final product," you are more likely to have to deal with plagiarism.

Deciding on a Thesis Statement

The thesis is the main idea, a proposition or statement to be proved. Written as part of the student's rough notes, it explains, in general terms, the purpose and/or scope of the essay.

A thesis statement is the main idea for the entire essay. Students who look up *thesis* in the dictionary will find something like "a proposition or statement to be proved." Some students may suggest that an older sibling or a parent has written a thesis for a degree—close but not quite what we're looking for.

I have tried to get my students to understand that the thesis for a given essay is the relatively specific topic that is being written about. It is not the biggest idea from the process of narrowing—"Sports" is not an essay thesis—nor is it the very specific ideas that form the main idea of a single paragraph. What it is—the *relatively specific* main idea for the essay, a statement that encompasses the main ideas dealt with in the body paragraphs.

1. It might come in the form of an opinion.

   Poverty is a problem right here in our city. I am convinced that we can provide some solutions.

   With this example, I remind my students that we have narrowed the topic of "poverty" down to the more specific idea of "poverty in our city," and suggest that the body paragraphs will deal with solutions that we can provide.

2. It might come in the form of a statement about a theme.

   Hypocrisy in government is threatening the freedom of everyone in our country.

   A major theme of "hypocrisy" has been narrowed to "hypocrisy in government." This particular essay will deal with how it is "threatening the freedom of all Canadians."

Exemplars—both the *emulating* and the *oops-here's-one-with-a-problem* type—can be very helpful. When I read a good thesis statement, I can tell what the essay is going to be about, and am able to suggest how the body paragraphs will support the thesis.

Teaching Tip

- It may help to use a slight twist on the pronunciation of the word "thesis." I suggest "this is." What I try to get my students to commit to is the notion that the thesis statement says "this is" what my essay is going to be about.
- If you have ever built a house (or a shed or a garage or whatever), you know that a square foundation is the key to everything that follows. Taking time to get students to understand the idea of a thesis is, metaphorically, laying the same foundation.

5 The Body of the Essay

When all is said and done, is more said than done?

When students are ready to write the body paragraphs of their essays, they can see the light at the end of the tunnel. All of the information has been gathered and ordered, and is just waiting to be put into paragraph form.

It may surprise students to find out that you are covering the body of the essay before the beginning of it (i.e., the introductory paragraph). But this is a good stage both to review paragraphing and to teach methods for students to use to write meaty and meaningful bodies for their essays.

Developmental Paragraphs

An essay is a series of paragraphs. We often assume that our students clearly understand what a paragraph is, and where topic sentences can be placed, but there is no better time than this to review. I draw the picture of a paragraph on the board (see page 54 for a version you can reproduce). Because this is a review, I ask class members to explain the various parts of a paragraph, including formatting, topic sentence, and concluding sentence.

Teaching Tip
• As a student explains a concept in answer to a question, move as far away from the speaker as possible. The theory is simple: if you can hear the "student teacher," so can everyone else.

Formatting

Paragraph formatting includes margins and indents.

Most students can do with a reminder that formatting does more than make a paragraph look nice. Aspects such as margins and indention really do contribute to how much sense the paragraph makes to the reader.

Picture of a Paragraph

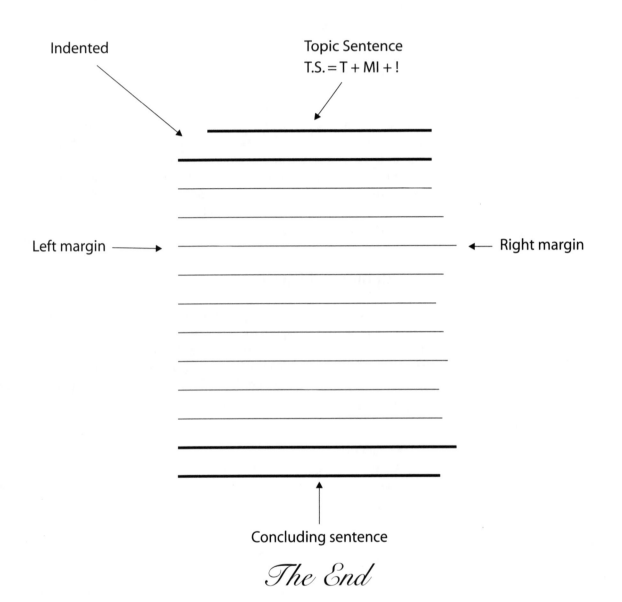

Indented

Topic Sentence
T.S. = T + MI + !

Left margin → ← Right margin

Concluding sentence

The End

Printers: students who do assignments in pen; may need to be reminded that others need to be able to decipher their writing

Rare subspecies: *Zigzagius profundi*: Printers whose left margins wander back and forth across the page

Word Processors: students who do everything on the computer; should be restricted to the print font/size of the teacher's choice

Indenters: students who indent each paragraph, as opposed to those who leave a line space between paragraphs

Indent: The debate of the day may seem to be whether to indent the first line of a new paragraph or to leave a space between paragraphs instead. With students, my concern is always consistency—that they choose one method and stick to it.

Right margin: The diagram shows that this is a staggered, crooked margin. Nevertheless, it is still a margin. I remind my Printers that they can use the red line showing through from the other side of the looseleaf paper as a guideline—the red line says "Stop!"—but that it doesn't have to be right on the red line, just somewhere nearby.

Left margin: I have encountered the *Zigzagius profoundi* only occasionally, and I have never been able to understand how such an obviously mistaken concept can remain a part of the student's writing repertoire for so long. I'm talking about the wandering left margin. When confronted to explain his (usually) or her creative approach to a marginal task, the only explanation I have received is a dreamy-eyed look followed by "Oh, I just kinda do it that way" or "What? You mean you're supposed to make it, like, totally straight?" If it's true that the devil is in the details, for some students, one of the small steps toward success is to start making the left margin straight.

Topic Sentence

> The topic sentence is a general statement that tells the reader what the paragraph is about. When placed first, it should interest or tempt the reader to continue.

My students would have been very happy to give titles to every paragraph. Up to Grade 8, most had not written anything much longer than a paragraph. Besides, coming up with titles was fun. Essays do not lend themselves to titles for every paragraph, so I found the following formula a good reinforcement of the idea that the topic sentence serves the same purpose.

T.S. = T + M.I. + !
Topic Sentence = Topic + Main Idea + Oomph

The idea that a paragraph has both a topic and a main idea is confusing to some. I attempt to explain by showing how the same topic can have multiple main ideas. I would ask them to suggest an exciting topic for, say, a descriptive paragraph. The suggestions (sometimes mine) would be things like my room, a cool car, the ultimate school desk, the perfect school lunch, the world's worst teacher, etc.

To explain the concept of the main idea, I would write the topic on the left-hand side of the board/overhead, then glean possible main ideas and list them in a column to the right:

	how messy it is
	all the neat stuff it has
my room	what I would like it to look like
	my side vs. my brother's side
	the good, the bad, and the ugly

The classroom never resounded with "Aha!"s when I first did this, but repeated examples seemed to get the idea across. The same topic could have multiple main ideas.

For those students who don't fully grasp either the formula or the single-topic-with-multiple-main-ideas concept, I simply said that the topic is *what the paragraph is about* and the main idea answers *what about the topic?* If the topic is "a cool car," then the main idea answers "Well, what about the cool car?" Are you going to tell us what special things the car has? Will you describe how the car matches your personality? Is it cool because you have added things to it?

Placement of the Topic Sentence

Many students will be successful if they include reasonable topic sentences as the first sentence of every paragraph. That said, I fear that we dummy down too often and fail to challenge the other students. Teaching them to vary the position of a topic sentence adds variety and interest.

The topic sentence as the second sentence is usually just the main idea following a sentence connecting it to the previous paragraph. Or it can be a topic sentence that has had a brief introduction. For example, if two adjoining paragraphs were about the costs of downhill skiing and the local opportunities for this exciting winter sport, the second paragraph might start like this:

> The facts are obvious; judicious money management is necessary in order to afford downhill skiing. But an abundance of opportunities, a veritable mountain of local moguls, awaits the recreational skier.

When saved until the end, the topic sentence can be climactic. The reader is kept (somewhat) in suspense as the author builds toward the actual topic and main idea. In an essay about a region of Scotland, a paragraph might end with, "And where in this favored land might someone find such a multi-dimensional place? The Kingdom of Fife!"

Oomph!

The idea of *oomph* is my favorite part of the whole topic sentence idea, and the one that seems to appeal most to students. I would often suggest that a perfectly acceptable topic sentence could consist of simply the topic and the main idea. I would give examples:

> My room is really messy.
> There is a lot of neat stuff in my room.
> I would like my room to look different.
> It's not hard to tell my side of the bedroom from my brother's side.
> My bedroom contains the good, the bad, and the ugly.

Some teachers will say, "You aren't going to hear my students using words like 'judicious' and 'veritable'!" Trust me. I just about dropped my coffee cup when a Grade 8 student commented, "To me it was just a case of 'Je ne sais quoi.'" It can happen.

Not only would I make the "acceptable" sentences look as boring as possible, I would say them in the most boring way possible, punctuated with yawns and eyes rolling.

To explain *oomph*, I use synonymous terms and related adjectives: *pizzazz, excitement, interest, attention-getting, electric*. I state that the easiest way to add oomph is to choose effective words. I do not suggest going to the thesaurus, just a quick visit to the brain (and sometimes a quick revisit to figurative language). We got results like these:

- My room looks like a tornado disaster area.
- If the Guinness Book of World Records had a "Neatest Stuff in a Kid's Room" category, my room would be the winner.
- Given enough money, I could give my room a makeover that would shock the world.
- If I were to describe my side of my room vs. my brother's side, start thinking of paradise vs. the dark side, the garden of Eden vs. the city dump, Disneyland vs. an elementary-school playground.
- As you enter the Reality Zone (my bedroom), know that you will encounter three things: the good, the bad, and the extremely ugly.

But ultimately we always have to come back to the fact that the topic sentence needs to state the topic and the main idea. Whether the sentences contained or lacked oomph, we double-underline the topic and single-underline the main idea in topic sentences whenever we can.

Concluding Sentence

> Like in the old movies, the concluding sentence says
>
> *The End*

In a stand-alone paragraph, the concluding sentence announces that the paragraph is finished, complete. In an essay, the concluding sentence is more likely to play the role of a transitional device, joining one paragraph to the next.

> **Teaching Tips**
> - You may find that, for the printing (as opposed to word-processing) sub-group of students who choose to indent, it works to suggest that the space to leave is the width of the thumb; some might buy into the tidy idea of five letter spaces.
> - The whole concept of a picture frame around an essay is best illustrated by holding up two handwritten examples for the class to see: one that has appropriate margins and one that doesn't.
> - The topic sentence is often placed first in the paragraph. The essay is a terrific place to show students that it can be placed as the second sentence, in the middle of the paragraph or even at the end.

Methods of Development

In my experience, and from the teachers I have spoken to while preparing this book, getting students to elaborate on ideas is one of the least successful aspects of teaching essay writing. Many students can create the structure but few build on it. As teachers, we end up looking at the basis of what could be good—but find the results often fall short.

Of course, practice helps. What also helps is having the Methods of Development right in front of our classes so that they can readily choose from the list of possibilities. I have found that creating an acronym helps. Having a rather odd-sounding acronym helps even more—"What do these FREQOES wanna hear in my essay that will help them remember my message?"

When developing an essay, you can use
- Facts and statistics
- Reasons
- Examples
- Quotes
- Opinions
- Experiences
- Senses

Facts and Statistics

Information that is truthful (a fact) or numerical data that has been collected (statistics) can make an argument more believable.

Fact: After high school I worked for a year before furthering my education.
Statistic: 68.3 % of statistics are made up.

Reasons

Tell the reader why, give some "becauses" with specific details.

If we had more recreational facilities we would have less crime. To begin with, young people would be busy having fun. They wouldn't have a lot of time on their hands and be so bored that they would go looking for trouble.

Examples

Support your belief with an illustration that provides more information.

One of the beauties of golf is that you can play at almost any age. At my course, there are kids like Andy Mack who is only seven, me at thirteen, my dad who is thirty-nine, and dad's friend, Archie McBean, who turned eighty last winter.

Quotes

Find someone who is knowledgeable about your topic and repeat exactly what he or she said to prove, explain, or clarify your point of view.

A Parliamentary Assistant to the MLA said, "A perfect example of hypocrisy right here in Canada came in 1993. Throughout his campaign, Jean Chrétien promised to get rid of the GST. That promise got him elected, but we're still paying 6% tax."

Opinions

Give your own view, judgment, or outlook.

> We can't blame the federal or the provincial government or someone else far away. I think that our local government is responsible for some of the recent problems dealing with street people.

Experiences

Tell about something that has happened in your life, or describe an event that you know has happened to someone else. It can be something that you saw happen, or it could be a short story (anecdote) about an incident that supports your point of view.

> I go to the hockey rink in winter and the in-line skating rink in summer. I am surrounded by healthy, active people who are having a great time. Nothing is perfect, but being involved in both kinds of hockey has been a positive experience for me and for lots of my friends.

Senses

Use sight, sound, smell, touch, and taste. Information in the body of the essay from the body of a person—i.e., visual, auditory, olfactory, tactile, or tastebudial —can assist in developing your ideas. Consider these examples from an essay about the process of self-discovery:

> *Visual*: At summer camp, we slept in real teepees. Our section had five huge canvas cones with wooden floors and rusty old army cots.
> *Auditory*: We awoke each morning to the raucous cries of birds.
> *Olfactory*: The sweet smell of the trees mixed with the lingering aroma of wood smoke.
> *Tactile*: My horse nuzzled me with his soft, velvety upper lip, and then rasped the remaining oats from the palm I had gingerly extended.
> *Taste*: Freshly picked, wild raspberries have a flavor and moistness that cannot be matched.

Teaching Tips
- Post the FREQOES acronym in the class in several places, for all to see and refer to. Have the students be the ones who create the acronym posters that adorn the walls and ceilings of the classroom.
- Go over them and over the methods of development. Put them on quizzes. Ask for the acronym and the seven words as an anticipatory set. Make giving you one of the methods an exit requirement. Have students jot the acronym vertically in the margin beside each body paragraph of an essay and circle the letters of any techniques used in that paragraph.
- Show students how these methods are effective in all kinds of situations.

---

6 Beginnings and Endings

You have only one chance to make a first, and lasting, impression.

As my wife says about any good meal, "It's all in the presentation!" Once the body paragraphs have been written, I work with my students on both the introductory and concluding paragraphs.

The Introductory Paragraph

> The Introductory Paragraph should prepare the reader for what is to follow and arouse the reader's interest in the topic.

In the pages that follow, you will find Type One exemplars (good models) for each type of introductory and concluding paragraph.

Because it is the first paragraph, logic would suggest that the introductory paragraph be written first. (Logic would also suggest that Panama hats are made in Panama; apparently they're made in Ecuador.) I ask my students to write the introductory paragraph as one of the last things they do.

I often show my classes a page from the classified ads. At a glance, the page looks like a gallimaufry of small print, ticky-tacky, same-same, hodgepodged Morse code. Closer inspection and perusal by the class prompts observations like, "Oh, there's one with a picture," "Some have got bold type," "Here's one that starts with 'Free'." The discussion underscores the idea that out of the chaos rises the phoenix of individuality, that some creative advertisers have made attempts to make their entries stand out.

> **Teaching Tips**
> - I offer exemplars as a way to get you started, but I encourage you to start you own collection from your own students.
> - Remember the thought about learning from "not-so-good" examples—truly "not-so-good" ones from years past and unidentified, or Type Two exemplars written specifically to be just that.

1. The Thesis Statement Alone

The introductory paragraph may consist of nothing more than a thesis statement. The Thesis Statement Alone opening has the advantage of brevity. Like

Apart from the Thesis Statement Alone, each type of introductory paragraph can include or add a thesis statement. The techniques should look like this:

- Personal Comment or Anecdote + Thesis Statement
- Questions +Thesis Statement
- Opposite View + Thesis Statement
- Quotation + Thesis Statement
- Startling Statement + Thesis Statement
- Mix + Thesis Statement

Another advantage of the personal comment or anecdote opening is that it provides a golden opportunity to set up the "cyclic return" (see page 72).

the short, punchy sentences that we suggest to students to get a short story off to a quick start, it has immediacy. A second advantage is clarity; there isn't anything in the way to cause confusion or ambiguity. Like the topic sentence (see page 56), it needs oomph or pizzazz to get the reader's attention.

> Against seemingly insurmountable odds, humans have shown an amazing will to survive. Three incredible people are evidence—one the victim of a head-on crash with a semi trailer, the second the survivor of a brain tumor, and the third the prey of a form of Lou Gehrig's Disease. *(from the essay "The Human Will to Survive" by Jerry W.)*

2. Personal Comment or Anecdote

The personal comment can be an opinion or statement about something that actually happened. An anecdote or brief story about something that has happened to the students or to someone they know can provide an excellent hook to catch the reader's attention. This type of opening adds authenticity and offers the opportunity for the essay writer to involve the reader.

Many of my students wouldn't know an anecdote from an antidote, or perhaps an anteater, when I first introduce the term. It is not likely that I can make things any clearer by discussing anecdotal records, so I have to just tell them what it is. The dictionary defines anecdote as "a short account of some interesting or amusing incident or event."

> Fast Eddie Riley did not just march to a different tune; he polkaed. I first met him in university residence. Bright but socially inept, friendly but friendless, and the unfortunate butt of jokes and pranks, I can remember clearly how much outside the norm he lived. *(from the essay "Individuals Who are Outsiders" by Pieter L.)*

3. Questions

An introductory paragraph can ask questions that will interest the reader. Whenever possible, they should be sequenced so that they suggest the order of the paragraphs in the body of the essay.

> Why would anyone ever want to wear a school uniform? What are the possible benefits of such a hair-brained scheme? Has such a plan ever been successful anywhere but some fancy-schmancy private school? My initial thoughts were: for no good reason, very few, and probably not. *(from the essay "Fit to be Tied" by Bruce A.)*

I have found it helpful to remind students of the 5W's and H. Unfortunately, this often leads to thinking "inside the box," as they offer up a series of questions, one per sentence. On the continuum of essay writing, initially I would be happy to get any kind of 5W's-and-H response. However, as students progress, I would hope that they would not follow the exact pattern of one *who* question, followed by one *what* question, and so on.

4. Opposite View

To arouse interest, an essay can begin with the exact opposite of the popular belief, or of the writer's real opinion. Afterwards, when the writer states his or her true point of view, the shock value can be an effective attention-getter.

Everyone knows that capital punishment, the death penalty, has been widely successful throughout the world. It has been performed by the most humane possible methods, it has deterred criminals from committing serious offences, and it is being adopted by more and more countries around the globe. Unfortunately, this is not the case. On the contrary, killing people for killing people doesn't work. *(from the essay "Capital Punishment: The Grave Reality" by Janet S.)*

5. Quotation

An appropriate quote may offer an effective beginning:

- It can state, in just a few words, the essence of what is to follow.
- It is often already known by the readers so it helps make a connection with past experience

"You can't build a reputation on what you are going to do." When Henry Ford, famous auto maker, made this statement, he backed it with performance. To build a reputation or to create anything substantial, the builder needs to begin with a dream, he has to set goals, and it helps if he has an ideal, a model, to imitate. Terry Fox was just such a builder. *(from the essay "The Influence of Dreams, Goals, and Ideals" by Robbie M.)*

It is important to get students to understand that it's the right quote in the right place that makes for an effective beginning. For me, the right quote often results from the "Poof" method. I use this term when describing the methods of finding rhyming words in our Poetry Unit: sometimes a good rhyming word just appears—*Poof!* It can be the same with finding the right quote to introduce an essay. If you understand the main point that you are trying to make, you may just be able to put your mind into Search mode and—*Poof!*—the appropriate quote will appear. Almost always, the quote needs to be tied to the topic so that the reader understands the connection.

For students, the Poof method may not work. Other sources do exist—try looking in books, surfing Internet sites, asking people. If possible, a quote should be attributed to the person who made it.

Students often struggle with the correct punctuation and capitalization when using quotes. The Using Quotes exercise on page 63 gives them some practice in incorporating quotes into their writing. I introduce the presentation of quotes in a series of anticipatory sets:

See the Quotes list on pages 64–65 for a smattering of quotes (including many of my personal favorites) from a variety of sources.

- opening quotations (the actual words appear first)
- closing quotations (the actual words appear last)
- divided quotations (speaker's words are divided by who the speaker is)
- indirect quotations (the exact words of a speaker are not given)

Using Quotes

Name: _____

In the box beside each of the following quotes, label it

- **O**—opening quotation (the actual words appear first)
- **C**—closing quotation (the actual words appear last)
- **D**—divided quotation (speaker's words are divided by who the speaker is)
- **I**—indirect quotation (the exact words of a speaker are not given)

Rewrite each quote in the space below, using correct capitalization and punctuation.

☐ I remember her saying something about the most sincere compliment you can pay is attention

☐ there are three kinds of people in this world those who can count and those who can't commented the wise man

☐ stand up for something he proposed or you will fall for everything

☐ gary player stated the harder you work the luckier you get

☐ i hear and I forget I see and I remember I do and I understand stated confucius

☐ sir edmund claimed the real reason that mountain climbers tie themselves together is so that the sensible one does not go home

☐ there is never a traffic jam noted our teacher on the extra mile

☐ generosity has been defined as giving away what you could use yourself

☐ change is inevitable growth is optional remarked the speaker

☐ beauty is only skin deep declared the clerk stupidity goes all the way through

☐ the senior citizen joked the older I get the better I was

☐ our lunchroom supervisor advised that if we weren't recycling that we were throwing it all away

Quotes

You can fool all of the people some of the time, and you can fool some of the people all of the time, but you can't fool all of the people all of the time. – Abe Lincoln

Some people don't exaggerate; they just remember BIG.

Too much of a good thing… is absolutely wonderful.

Out of the mouths of babes often come things adults should never have said in the first place.

Long walks are great, especially when they are taken by people who are annoying.

Contentment is the smother of invention. —Laura Watson

You may be too old to be young, but you're never too old to be immature.

Are you here to do something, or are you here for something to do?

May you be the kind of person your dog thinks you are. —Mahatma Dahji

It's not the size of the dog in the fight; it's the size of the fight in the dog.

Less is more. —Ludwig Mies van der Rohe

He is from the "Ready, Shoot, Aim" school of thought.

There are three kinds of people: those who make things happen, those who watch things happen, and those who sit around and wonder, "What happened?"

There are four stages in teaching: the unconscious incompetent, the conscious incompetent, the conscious competent, the unconscious competent.

The only time a fisherman tells the truth is when he calls other fishermen liars.

What I know about that would fill a thimble and leave room for a bag lunch.

I let my mind wander and it didn't come back.

Take turns with the things you neglect. —Donna Mackenzie

I don't understand all I know about that. —Fred Moore

It's too bad that all of the people who know how to run the country are busy driving cabs and cutting hair. —George Burns

Eagles may soar but weasels don't get sucked into jet engines. —Nick Flugaur

Duct tape is like the Force. It has a light side and a dark side and it holds the universe together. —Carl Zwanzig

Quotes (cont'd.)

Always remember that you are unique—just like everyone else. —Alison Boulter

Experience is the worst teacher. It gives the test before presenting the lesson. —Vernon Law

The first rule of wise financial management is to save something for a rainy day; the second, to distinguish between light sprinkles and heavy showers. —Harry Karns

You can't build a reputation on what you are going to do. —Henry Ford

If you think you can do a thing or think you can't do a thing, you're right. —Henry Ford (attributed)

History is more or less bunk. It's tradition. We don't want tradition. We want to live in the present and the only history worth a tinker's damn is the history we made today. —Henry Ford

Human beings are the only creatures on earth that allow their children to return home. —Bill Cosby

Learning is not compulsory . . . neither is survival. —W. Edwards Deming

A teacher is one who makes himself progressively unnecessary. —Thomas Carruthers

One can succeed at almost anything for which he has enthusiasm. —Charles Schwab

You have to expect things of yourself before you can do them. —Michael Jordan

Luck is what happens when preparation meets opportunity. —Coach Darrel Royal

We learn from history that we do not learn from history. —G.W. F. Hegel

No one goes there nowadays; it's too crowded. —Yogi Berra

Baseball is 90% mental; the other half is physical. —Yogi Berra

If the fans don't come out to the ballpark, no one can stop 'em. —Yogi Berra

You can observe a lot by just watching. —Yogi Berra

One hundred per cent of the shots you don't take won't go in. —Wayne Gretzky

The Introductory Paragraph: Student Notes

This paragraph should prepare the reader for what is to follow and arouse the reader's interest in the topic.

Types of Introductory Paragraphs

1. Thesis Statement

A thesis statement is the main idea for the entire essay. Because a thesis statement is usually only one sentence, some further explanation is required in the introductory paragraph. Identifying the main subsections of the essay and noting the order in which they will appear is helpful to the reader.

2. Personal Comment or Anecdote

The personal comment can be an opinion or a statement about something that actually happened. An anecdote or brief story about something that has happened to you or to someone you know can provide an excellent hook to catch the reader's attention.

3. Questions

Ask questions that will interest the reader and, whenever possible, sequence them so that they suggest the order of the paragraphs in the body of the essay.

4. Opposite View

To arouse interest, begin with the exact opposite of the popular belief, or of your real opinion. Afterwards, state your true point of view. The shock value can be an effective attention-getter.

5. Quotation

An appropriate quote may offer an effective beginning. Choosing the right length is important. A short quote can be explained or elaborated, a medium length quote may be just right, but a long one is likely to be just that—too long.

6. Startling Statement

Rock 'em, sock 'em, and shock 'em! Grab the reader's attention with an outlandish statement. Surprise the reader with something out of the ordinary.

7. The Mix

You can weave an introductory paragraph from a blend of the techniques described above. With a little of this and little of that, the results should be creative, descriptive, interesting, and informative.

Introductory Paragraphs Exercise

Name: _____

On these lines, write the seven methods you have studied for writing introductory paragraphs.

_____   _____

_____   _____

_____   _____

_____

Below each introductory paragraph, write the name of the technique that has been used.

1. Where does the light go when the light goes out? Who put the bomp in the bomp bah bomp bah bomp? Who put the ram in the rama lama ding dong? How do they get the caramel in the Cadbury chocolate bar? Do you have an inquiring mind but can't find answers? Research using the "People You Know" method, the "People Who Know The People You Know" method, and, of course, effective use of the Internet will provide positive results.

_____

2. Successful salesman and Scottish entrepreneur, Tommy Dewar, once stated, "Fish stimulates the brain, but fishing stimulates the imagination." Imagination is the cornerstone of creativity. The craving for creativity can be satisfied only if you are willing to take risks, to picture life from varying points of view, and to think outside the bag.

_____

3. It has been said that some are born great, some achieve greatness, and some have greatness thrust upon them. But mirror, mirror, on the wall, who's the greatest of them all? In the mystifying and mythical world of the Greeks, is it Heracles, Odysseus, or Achilles? Each has his claim to fame.

_____

Introductory Paragraphs Exercise (cont'd)

4. One person just can't do that much! Poverty surrounds us and there isn't that much that a teenager can do… or is there? I believe that by starting small, by setting an example, and by sharing your successes, you really can accomplish something.

_____

5. The theme of justice runs throughout *The Merchant of Venice*. To appreciate what William Shakespeare's play, written over 400 years ago, has to say to us today, consideration should be given to the letter of the law, "legal" versus "just," and justice for all.

_____

6. My life is in the toilet. I've been dealt such a rotten hand it's a miracle how I even survive. Thinking like this is counterproductive. The world of entertainment is filled with examples of people who battled adversity and won. Orphan James Michener, stutterer Mel Tillis, and one-eyed Sammy Davis Junior are three examples.

_____

7. We called him Black Bart. He wore a black cowboy hat, a black T-shirt, black jeans and black trucker boots—and he carried a hunting knife on his belt. He used to throw the knife into the wall of the mess hall each night before supper. Every kid in camp was afraid of him, that is, until rock climbing school. We all learned three things at camp that year—fear is blinding, all is not as it appears, and revenge is bittersweet.

_____

6. Startling Statement

Rock 'em, sock 'em, and shock 'em! An essay can immediately grab the reader's attention with an outlandish statement, the height of hyperbole. The writer can exaggerate, embellish, amplify, and inflate. The essay reader, generally, is expecting a more formal, logical argument or explanation than what might be found in a story or poem; the essay writer can surprise the reader with something incongruous.

Golf is gaining popularity faster than *any* summer sport! Thanks to superstars like Tiger Woods giving personal lessons to kids right here in our town, and thanks to millions of dollars in golf scholarships being given out in our own school, and even bigger thanks to the fact that new studies show that golfers, on average, live twenty years longer than other athletes. Well, perhaps these are slightly exaggerated statements, but golf is a great sport. The stars of the sport, the possibilities for a great career, and the physical benefits help make golf a big hit. *(from the essay "Golf" by Robert R.)*

7. The Mix

Teachers have complained to me that they are tired of the "cookie cutter" responses that they get from too many students in too many essays. What we, as teachers, are striving for is to get our charges to go to their toolboxes, to select from the array of tools that we have given them (or that we have collected together), and then to build something unique.

Students can weave an introductory paragraph from a blend of the techniques described here. With a little of this, and little of that, the results should be creative, descriptive, interesting, and informative.

Curfews. When all else fails, adults revert to rules. The rules don't have to make sense. They don't have to be easy to enforce. They just have to sound simple. Once again, adolescents are faced with the threat from the "Ready, Shoot, Aim" school of thought. What's the real problem? How did we get here? Where should we really be looking for answers? *(from the essay "Curfews" by Pat M.)*

Once you have gone over the different types of introductory paragraphs with your class, you can use the Introductory Paragraphs Exercise on pages 67–68 to reinforce their learning.

Answer Key:

1. Questions
2. Quote
3. Mix
4. Opposite View
5. Thesis Statement
6. Startling Statement
7. Personal Comment or Anecdote

Teaching Tips

- Encourage students to see the introductory paragraph as perhaps the most enjoyable part of the essay. This is their chance to promote their product, to say "Pick me; pick me!"
- When using a quotation-based introductory paragraph, choosing the right length of quote is important. Remember "Goldilocks and the Three Bears": a short quote might need to be explained or elaborated, a medium-length quote may be just right, but a long one is likely to be just that—too long.
- With each of the techniques, other than the Thesis Statement Alone, it is possible (and probably advisable) to add a thesis statement to the introductory paragraph. The techniques should look like this: Personal Comment or Anecdote + Thesis Statement, Questions +Thesis Statement, Opposite View + Thesis Statement, etc.

- Emphasize to students that the thesis statement is not necessarily tacked on at the end of the introductory paragraph. With a little creativity, there may be other ways to include the thesis in the paragraph.
- There are several ways you can use The Introductory Paragraph: Student Notes on page 66. You can go over the material in class and hand out the notes, or have students copy them from an overhead or from dictation. You can even create a cloze exercise from the notes.

The Concluding Paragraph

The purpose of the final paragraph is to bring the essay to a smooth conclusion. Similar to the last page in a children's book, or at the end of an old movie, it is a way of saying

The End

A strong finish can be as important as a strong opening. In her book *Reading and Language Arts Worksheets Don't Grow Dendrites*, Marcia Tate reminds us,

A brain concept called the theory of *primacy and recency* states that the brain pays closest attention to the first thing it hears in a learning segment and pays second closest attention to the last thing it hears.

As teachers, we need to encourage our students to finish with a BANG! If the essay were a short story, the concluding paragraph would be the denouement, the resolution. The final paragraph needs to tie up the loose ends, to answer any unanswered questions. In some cases, the conclusion can be even more than an effective and definite ending; it can suggest what should or could happen next.

The concluding paragraph is usually shorter than the body paragraphs, often only three to five sentences. In some instances, this final paragraph will start with a word or phrase that signals that the end is near: *In conclusion, Now, Finally, It should now be clear*, etc.

Just as there are many forms of the introductory paragraph, there are several techniques that can be used in an effective concluding paragraph.

If the concluding paragraph is at the bottom of a page, the reader should not be tempted to turn the page—it should be perfectly obvious that the essay is done.

1. Restating the Main Points

Remember the definition of the essay that deals with "Telling 'em" (page 9)? The concluding paragraph can be the "Tell 'em what you told 'em" part. It can restate the key ideas, but using different wording. You have to help students see that the idea is to be repetitive in a productive way, not a redundant one.

If it is your habit to begin many of your classes with an explanation of what the objectives of the lesson are, and then, at the end of the class, to summarize the main points, your students should have no trouble catching on to this technique. The challenge is to say the same thing but not the same way.

Introductory paragraph: It may be helpful to understand the equipment that is required to go scuba diving. Of equal importance is a basic knowledge of safety measures. Finally, it may be nice to know the location of nearby places where the awesome sport of scuba diving can be enjoyed.

Concluding paragraph: So before heading out to enjoy the great sport of scuba diving, remember to get the proper clothing and gear, and to follow the list of "Do's and Don'ts." Somewhere nearby there is an underwater adventure just waiting to be enjoyed. *(from the essay "Scuba Diving" by Tibor S.)*

2. The Future/Suggestions for Action

The end of an essay may be the most suitable time to discuss what should happen next. Depending on the topic, it may be appropriate for the essay writer to do some prognosticating about what the future may bring, or to suggest that the reader, having acquired newfound knowledge offered in the essay, could seek even further information.

This technique could bear yet another title—The Tip of the Iceberg. Inquiring minds, whose interest has been piqued, are likely to desire more data. The writer can take advantage of the teachable moment and offer some suggestions.

The NIMBY (Not In My Back Yard) idea could be much more than an idea in your life. We are all going to die. How we die is open for discussion. Now that you know about a living will and a personal directive, and have heard the true life—and death—stories of two real people, what choices do you have to make? *(from the essay "Euthanasia" by Gurpreet K.)*

3. Questions

Whether or not questions were used in the introduction, they can be used in the conclusion. If they were used in the introduction, more can be asked in the conclusion. If they were not used to start, the end is a perfect time for students to try this technique. Basically rhetorical in nature, questions serve a similar purpose to the previous technique. They offer a springboard for the reader to seek more information about the topic, or at least to think about what lies ahead.

I believe that my students are aware of rhetorical questions. Every day, as each student enters the classroom, I am met with statements like, "Good morning, Mr. Mackenzie. What can I do today to make your day a little brighter and your teacher load just a bit easier?"

In conclusion, it should be obvious that why we take risks, who is responsible for the results, and when it is reasonable to put our lives on the line is a very personal set of questions. The most important question of all remains: In that split second when a major decision is required, will you have the foresight and the will power to do what you know is the right thing to do? *(from the essay "Risk Taking" by Andrew S.)*

4. Personal Comment or Anecdote

Perhaps the best use of this technique is completing a comment or anecdote that was begun in the introduction at the end of the essay.

Once again, if this technique wasn't used in the introductory paragraph it makes an effective conclusion. If the essay writer used it earlier, the comment or anecdote can be reworded.

> As we saw at the outset, Jane Doe had a big decision—one that affected her life, her baby's life, and the lives of countless others around her. In this case, Jane kept the baby. It has been a story of triumph, of tears, of hopes, of sacrifice, of loneliness, of joy, and it will continue to be a life of wondering. Did I make the right decision? (from the essay "Abortion" by Jillian K.)

5. Cyclic Return

With the exception of The Future/ Suggestions for Action technique, all the others may use the cyclic return, at least in part.

The cyclic return performs the function of returning to the beginning of the cycle. The cyclic return is the tidy denouement. It ties up the loose ends by tying a nice bow on our gift to our readers. The essay writer reminds the reader where this particular journey began. The main points may be restated, questions asked initially may be answered, a story begun may be finished, a quote given may be followed up with a comment.

> So where does that leave us? It seems to take us back to where we started—like someone lost in the woods returning the original campsite. We still have the same questions, we still have the same barriers, and we still have the same dress code. Will it ever change? My money says it won't. Hey, there goes an airborne sow! (from the essay "School Dress Code" by Jeremy J.)

Once you have gone over the different types of introductory paragraphs with your class, you can use the Concluding Paragraphs Exercise on page 74 to reinforce their learning.
Answer Key:
1. Cyclic Return
2. The Future/Suggestions for Action
3. Personal Comment or Anecdote
4. Questions
5. Restating the Main Idea

Teaching Tips
- When teaching students to restate the main points, ask them to reword old sayings or morals. "It's hard to teach an old dog new tricks" becomes "It is difficult to indoctrinate a superannuated canine with innovative maneuvers." You can also try slogans from advertising.
- There are several ways you can use The Concluding Paragraph: Student Notes on page 73. You can go over the material in class and hand out the notes, or have students copy them from an overhead or from dictation. You can even create a cloze exercise from the notes.

The Concluding Paragraph: Student Notes

The purpose of the final paragraph is to bring the essay to a smooth conclusion. Similar to the last page in a children's book, or at the end of an old movie, it is a way of saying, "The End!"

Words and phrases that signal that the end is near:

Accordingly	It should now be clear
As a result	On the whole
As I have shown	Now
Consequently	Summing up
Finally	Therefore
Hence	Thus
In brief	To conclude
In conclusion	To sum up
In consequence	

Types of Concluding Paragraphs

1. Restating the Main Points
Restate the key ideas, but use different wording. The challenge is to say the same thing but not the same way.

2. The Future/Suggestions for Action
Discuss what should happen next. Depending on the topic, you might do some guessing about what the future may bring, or suggest that the reader could seek even further information.

3. Questions
Whether or not "questions" were used in the introduction, they can be used in the conclusion. If they were used, more can be asked. If they were not used to start, the end is a perfect time.

4. Personal Comment or Anecdote
If this technique wasn't used in the introductory paragraph it makes an effective conclusion. If it was used earlier, it can be reworded. Perhaps best of all is the technique of completing the comment or anecdote at the end of the essay.

5. Cyclic Return
The cyclic return performs the function of returning to the beginning of the cycle. The essay writer reminds the reader where this particular journey began. The main points may be restated, questions asked initially may be answered, a story begun may be finished, a quote given may be followed up with a comment.

Concluding Paragraphs Exercise

Name: _____

Certain skills are required to write the types of conclusions you have studied. Beneath each skill listed below, write the "type of conclusion" for which that skill is best suited:

1. Being able to complete a circle, or to return to the place where you began.

   _____

2. Thinking of ways to get the reader involved in doing something after reading the essay.

   _____

3. Sharing a real-life experience or telling a story to help sum up your topic.

   _____

4. Asking the reader to do something or to think about something.

   _____

5. Saying what you have already said but in different words.

   _____

7 After Writing

It ain't over 'til it's over. —Yogi Berra

In my early years in teaching, whenever I heard the term "revising," it was followed by its seeming partner-for-life "editing." I thought they were synonymous. As a child, I thought *lmn* was a letter. When we sang the Alphabet Song, it sounded like that to me: …h-i-j-k-lmn-o-p…" Surprise, surprise! I was wrong on both counts.

Revising

Revising is the process of checking an essay for the "big ideas." The author looks at his or her work to determine whether or not the essay says what it was intended to say. Is there enough information? Too much? Are the ideas arranged in the best possible order? Is there anything that should be added, deleted, or changed?

In a perfect world, incubation time may be possible. I think it's a little bit like telling married couples never to go to bed mad. Are you married? See my point? Not married? Trust me.

It has been suggested that once an essay has been written, it should be set aside for a period of time. Time to incubate is supposed to allow the author a chance for a mental holiday, a period of respite, so that he or she can view the writing from a fresh perspective. The incubation period, in reality, might be long enough to get another cup of coffee. The point is that the essay needs to be reread by the author, who is looking at it in the grand scheme. There's no sense correcting spelling mistakes that aren't going to appear in the final version. The idea is to read it over carefully to see if you like the whole package.

COAD Method

As teachers, we want to help students in their quest for clear communication— in particular, as the students write essays. If a student is willing to revise, to see again, then we are lucky. I suggest providing them with a simple checklist (see COAD Checklist for Revising on page 77):

- Is there anything that I could Change? (word choice, sentence length)
- Is the Order effective?
- Is there enough information? Should I Add anything?
- Is there too much information? Should I Delete some things?

Have students ask themselves the simple question: Is my essay up to COAD? I would be happy to have students accept the fact that four simple questions can mean the difference between clearly explaining a series of ideas and wasting an inordinate amount of time to create a substandard product, that revision is one of final steps in an important journey, not a chance to rewrite in one's best handwriting or re-keyboard in some interesting font.

Legend and Color Method

Another revision method that seems to have considerable merit is one described to me by high-school English teacher Lisa Robertson. It works like this:

1. Each student is given three or four pencil crayons from a class collection.
2. Each student then creates a legend. If the student got blue, pink, red, and green, then the legend might be

   blue = topic & concluding sentences
   pink = main points
   red = evidence & examples
   green = thesis statement

3. Each student goes about "coloring" the essay to match the legend. A blue box would go around the topic and concluding sentence in each paragraph; underlining would be used for the other items.

When the revision process is complete, every sentence should have a color. Lack of color indicates a problem. It's clear for the student to see what needs revision. Careful revision will create a coherent essay. Some extra attention is required for both order and coherence.

Lisa also uses the Legend and Color method after she has marked the rough copy of a student's essay. For a student who disagrees with Lisa's assessment, she can ask that that student perform a Legend and Color check. Once the student has double-checked to see if the required elements have been included, there is seldom further cause for concern.

Order

Students often overlook the concept of order. It does not seem to occur to them that they can revise the order of their ideas to be more effective. For those who do spend a few minutes thinking about the sequence of their ideas, they often fall back on one of the few techniques that they are aware of—chronological order.

Making choices about order can begin with the scattergram or by the student simply being aware that order is important and making a mental note to choose appropriately. It goes back to the idea of working smarter, not harder. In the scattergram, numbering the ideas before writing them into sentences is often an efficient method (see pages 34–35). But what are the alternatives?

Time (Chronological) Order

Time or chronological order is often choice #1. For example, in a paragraph about Terry Fox overcoming challenges in early life, students decide to begin with events that occurred in his pre-school days, followed by a Grade 8 experience, followed by an obstacle that he overcame in high school.

Reverse time order is another option: the writer goes from the present to the most recent event of the past, then the next most recent, and so on, dealing with incidents traveling back along a time line.

COAD Checklist for Revising

Essay Title: _____ Name: _____

❑ Is there anything that I could **C**hange? (word choice, sentence length)

_____

_____

_____

_____

❑ Is the **O**rder effective?

_____

_____

_____

_____

❑ Is there enough information? Should I **A**dd anything?

_____

_____

_____

_____

❑ Is there too much information? Should I **D**elete some things?

_____

_____

_____

_____

Building Order of Importance

The author uses this technique to build toward a climax. This strategy can be used in ordering a paragraph or an entire essay. A good fact is followed by a better one, then an even better one, and finally the best one. While this is touted as being a particularly effective method, I find it too predictable. My preference is a mix of facts, ideas, and supportive material that may generally build upwards, but does so in a fashion that is more logical than predetermined. Nevertheless, the order of importance concept is a good strategy for beginners and gives them a solid technique to store in their toolboxes.

Most Obvious to Least Obvious

The most-to-least-obvious order flies in the face of building suspense, or laying the groundwork and leading up to the "Aha!" moment at the end.

This order looks at the Big Picture and then the details. Within a paragraph, if the topic sentence has come first, the reader knows the topic and the main idea of that paragraph. The author can then support the main idea with specific details. In an essay, a thesis statement can explain the author's main idea or proposition and then support it with the most obvious arguments, followed by ones that are less so. Think about a defence presented in court: the accused who pleads not guilty has given the jury the big picture, and the lawyer's job is then to prove the claim.

Known-to-New

Certainly a wise choice if the essay is persuasive in nature, is going from known to new. The author may begin with familiar material that gets the reader in agreement mode. New information is gradually added to build on the known.

Simple-to-Complex

Quite similar to known-to-new is the simple-to-complex technique. The author establishes a base of concepts that are easily understood, and then develops, by whatever degree is felt to be appropriate, increasingly complex ideas.

A Chosen Pattern

When none of the above techniques seem appropriate, it is still possible to determine some system of order, if only for the reason that having a pattern to follow makes things clearer for the reader. Alphabetical order is an obvious choice. All else being equal, the author could decide that any accepted system could serve as a method of order: numeric (odd and even, smallest to largest), color, size, shape, etc.

Coherence

When it comes to reading the good copies of essays that my students have written, I often feel as I do at the end of the school year. I have mixed emotions. In June, when students sign my yearbook or are kind enough to present me with a card, it is not uncommon to see something like this: *Your the best!*

As I read the essays, I am assaulted with series of ideas that are not truly incoherent, yet don't qualify for top marks in the coherence category. I don't think that kids understand "coherence." Perhaps a good way to get them to understand the concept would be to spend more time explaining it. And one good way to spend that time might be to emphasize the opposite—incoherence.

Try mumbling the instructions for the day. "Good morning, ladies and genelmum. Today we will be esambling the essenshumal diffren beswan claristy and prombelashation." You are likely (I hope) to be met with at least someone who will say, "Pardon me? I don't understand what you're saying."

Your response? "Oh, I'm sorry. I was being incoherent, unclear, unintelligible, and disjointed. In this case, I was not enunciating clearly. My message wasn't getting through. If that is what incoherence is, then coherence is the opposite—being clear, intelligible, and joined smoothly; having everything together so that it makes sense."

Another way of helping our students come to an understanding of coherence is to have them use a knowledge of root words to determine unknown meanings. In the case of "coherence" it helps to know what the prefix "co-" means. I have the students jot down words they know that start with "co-": *cooperate* (If you and I cooperate, we will get done faster), *cosign* (My parents will cosign the loan so I can buy a car), *coexist* (The two countries were able to coexist after the war). I help them realize that "co-" has something to do with togetherness.

When asked for words that are similar to "coherent," they might jot down *inherent, cohesive, adhesive, adherent.* Maybe. They might know that if someone has an inherent quality—like inherent honesty—that quality is a natural part of their makeup. Maybe. They might think of adhesive tape and know that it is sticky. Maybe.

For those who don't get it, you may simply have to say that "coherent" and "adhere" have the same Latin root: *haerere,* or "to stick." Coherence means that the ideas *stick together.*

As we focus on coherence at the essay writing stage, it is crucial to demonstrate coherence between paragraphs. As the essay is divided into paragraphs, the main ideas of the paragraphs are different. At the same time, there must be some relationship. To display coherence, the writer must assist the reader in seeing this connection.

Using Joining Words/Transitional Devices

When you think back to the picture of an essay on page 10, you will remember the arrows that showed the connection from one paragraph to the next. Often a transitional word or phrase can aid in joining ideas, in creating a smooth flow—see the lists of Joining Words (page 81) and Transitional Devices (page 82) for some suggestions.

I used to ask my students to describe, in point form, a task that a Kindergarten child might have trouble performing. We brainstormed things like tying shoelaces, getting dressed for a winter recess, wrapping a present. We printed out the lists (in large print) and then delivered them to one of our feeder schools. The Kindergarten students, obviously with assistance, wrote back to critique the lists. This set the scene for the "work" part of the project. Adding the appropriate joining words /transitional devices, my students then wrote out the sequences in paragraph form for a middle-school audience.

Those of you who have taught a student with autism know what disjointed is like. One minute you can be involved in a conversation on the topic of the day, and the next minute it's a side trip about fighter planes or weight loss.

All of the words on the list of Joining Words (page 81) appear on the list of Transitional Devices (page 82). The longer list is offered for either higher grades, or for students who can handle terms like *vis à vis, allegedly, to substantiate.*

Other exercises using joining words:

- Have students think of things that need to be done in a sequence. Get them to write the steps down in a scrambled order. After trading lists with class-mates, they rewrite the steps in the proper sequence and add joining words. Some possibilities: How to be a Friend, Impressing Someone of the Opposite Sex, Preparing for the Big Test, Getting Your Driver's Licence, How to be Cool, Avoiding Homework.
- Have students watch a TV program. They retell (not "write" but "tell") the events in the order they occurred—with the aid of the Joining Words list (page 81). Repeating the same joining word is not allowed.
- Challenge students to perform a task for the class (or a small group). In preparation, the student should include at least one term from each group of words on the list of Joining Words (page 81). Some possibilities: performing a magic trick; showing how to make a "string game" figure; making something using origami; explaining how to draw an animal.

Teaching Tips

- Students might be a little shaky with their Latin derivations, and their understanding of prefixes and suffixes, but we often don't give them enough credit for being able to figure things out. Try to get students to avoid a trip to the dictionary by looking first at what is right in front of them. When they run across a difficult word, suggest that they think of any other words that look or sound similar—and to jot them down. It's even better if they can think of how the list words might be used in a sentence. By comparing what they do know with what they don't know, sometimes the light goes on and they discover that they are capable of determining meaning all by themselves.
- Once your students have a better understanding of what coherence means, show them some examples of both incoherent and coherent writing.

Editing

I used to think that revising and editing were the same thing because they were always mentioned together—like love and marriage, popcorn and a movie, pizza and beer. I can see now that there is a difference. I can also appreciate that, in some instances, two words that are commonly used together are indicative of an order; i.e. first the author revises, then the author edits.

Editing is the process of checking the mechanics of writing; for example, spelling, punctuation, capitalization, subject–verb agreement.

In the writing process, editing is usually seen as the last stage before creation of the good or final copy. I try to suggest to students that some editing can be done *during* the writing process. For me, the moment that I first write a word is the time that I question whether or not I am spelling it correctly. I encourage students to commit to the fact that it is at this precise moment that the student should stop in mid-thought, grab the huge dictionary perched precariously on the corner of the desk, and check the spelling. Just kidding. While the thought process is far more important at the early stage of writing, it does take only a millisecond to underline the word in question.

A word may be spelled correctly; it may not. The millisecond taken to underline it is well spent because the potentially misspelled word has been highlighted and can be checked later.

Joining Words

Time/Sequence

after

before

finally

first

following this

in the first place

later

next

now

once

previously

second, third, *etc.*

since

then

to begin with

until

when

while

To Qualify

except

generally

often

usually

Comparison

by comparison

equally

in the same way

likewise

similarly

Contrast

although

alternatively

but

however

in contrast

instead

on the other hand

otherwise

Proof

because

evidently

for example

for instance

obviously

since

Addition

also

and

besides

equally important

furthermore

in addition

in other words

Exception

despite

in spite of

nevertheless

sometimes

Conclude

as a result

as I have shown

in brief

in conclusion

on the whole

so

therefore

thus

to conclude

to sum up

Transitional Devices

Time/Sequence
after
afterward
and then
at this point
at this time
before
concurrently
consequently
finally
first
following this
formerly
given that…then
hence
immediately
in the first place
later
next
now
once
previously
second, third, *etc.*
simultaneously
since
subsequently
then
thereafter
to begin with
until
when
while

To Qualify
allegedly
except
generally
often
specifically
usually

Comparison
by comparison
compared to
equally
in the same way
like
likewise
similarly
vis à vis

Contrast
although
alternatively
but
conversely
however
in contrast
instead
meanwhile
on the contrary
on the other hand
otherwise
rather
whereas
yet

Proof
because
besides
evidently
for example
for instance
for the same reason
in any case
in fact
obviously
since
that is
to confirm
to establish
to justify
to show
to substantiate
to verify

Addition
above all
again
also
and
besides
equally important
furthermore
in addition
in other words
moreover
what's more
too

Exception
despite
in spite of
nevertheless
once in a while
sometimes
still

Conclude
accordingly
as a result
as I have shown
consequently
finally
hence
in brief
in conclusion
in consequence
in short
on the whole
so
summing up
therefore
thus
to conclude
to sum up

Concession
granted that
it is true that

The Mackenzie Snake

I find that a systematic, active approach to editing is most useful. This particular technique received its name because I invented it (I think), and because the process is one that sees student essays snake their way around the classroom.

Because editing is not the most exciting part of writing an essay, I have tried to follow my grandmother's advice: "Many hands make light work." When the deadline for having the rough copy of the essay has arrived, I check with the class to see who is ready for editing and who is not. Those who are not ready sit at one end of the room and work to complete their essays. The ones who are done (surprisingly, always the majority) sit in the remaining desks.

I then devise a pattern that snakes up and down the rows of students: the first student in the first row hands his/her paper back, the other students in the row follow suit; the last student in the row hands his/her paper across to the student in the next row; the students in the second row hand their papers forward; the person at the front of the second row hands his/her paper across to the person in the next row, and the papers are passed back. A snake pattern is established and papers are handed from one student to the next. The only person with an onerous task is the student at the end of the snake, whose job is to take each paper, once finished a stage of editing, to the person at the front of the snake.

Logic would suggest that the hyperactive, likes-a-lot-of-movement student would be best suited to be the Pony Express rider at the end of the snake. Reality suggests that a well-behaved, quiet student can better enjoy this moment of being helpful and appreciated.

Once the snaking has been established, editing can begin. I ask the editors to look for one thing at a time; e.g., spelling. If they think a word is misspelled in the essay they are editing, they simply write *Sp* above it. When I call "Switch," each student passes the paper on to the next editor, who also checks for spelling. After several passes and spelling checks, I ask that some other check be made.

An advantage of this system is that students of varying abilities check a number of papers. Stronger academic students may be more helpful as editors while weaker academic students may get more than they give. By reading the work of others, these weaker students may learn things that they wouldn't in editing their own work. At the same time, they may have certain areas of expertise that allow them to help peers who are generally seen as better writers—but not better in all aspects of writing. All students get to read what their classmates have written.

In my experience, as important as choosing a set of basic proofreader's marks is agreeing to agree with the rest of your school on a standard set everyone can (and hopefully will) use. Do your students a favor—standardize!

It is critical to agree on how to indicate editing. Editing, done by students, is "an opinion"; therefore, it should be done in pencil. It helps if the rough copy has been double-spaced with margins on both sides, allowing room for editing. The teacher has to decide on the system to use to indicate what the student editor "thinks" is an error. See page 85 for a generally accepted list of proofreader's marks.

The Pencil and Symbol Method

High-school teacher Lisa Robertson uses pencils and symbols to help students edit their own essays. At the beginning of the term, students follow her instructions as she leads them through a variety of editing steps. Step 1 might be to put an X over every example of abbreviated speech: "MSN" language such as "u" for *you*, "i" for *I*, "4" instead of *for*. Step 2 might be to underline every contraction. Step 3 could be to circle words that the student editor believes are misspelled. Personal pronouns could be boxed, too general terms like "stuff" could be double-underlined. Later in the term, given a list of what to edit for, students can edit their own papers.

I give my students the marking key for the assignment in advance. Those students who care to see what is being emphasized on a particular assignment can then emphasize it in their editing.

After some peer editing has been completed, the essay is returned to the author. It is then the author's job to determine which of the helpful suggestions requires correction.

Teaching Tips

- Have students try reading a piece of writing backwards when checking for spelling. The idea is that seeing a word in isolation allows them to concentrate on whether or not it is spelled correctly, and they are less likely to get caught up in the flow of ideas.
- What happens when a paper is checked over and over by editors who start (where most would) at the beginning? The longer papers would never have the latter portions edited. Ask that students initial, in the margin, where they are when you call them to switch papers. This gives the next editor a starting point.
- Students as editors are only truly worthwhile if they are capable. Use this opportunity for some mini-lessons. Before checking for capitalization, do a little tune-up. Before checking for consistent verb tense, present some examples—good and bad. Students generally react positively to these reminders because they have an immediate purpose.
- When editing for spelling, underline the part of the word that is mis<u>schp</u>elled. This aids kids in knowing what to look for when they try to make corrections. For example, if a student has misspelled *concentrate* as "connsintrait," he or she can quite easily find it by skimming the "con-" section in the dictionary, knowing that the error was in the "-nsintrait" part of the word.

Proofreader's Marks

¶ or *par*	new paragraph
∧	insert
ℓ	delete
om	omitted word
sp	spelling error
p	punctuation error
≡ (triple underline)	capital letter
/ (slash)	lower case
var	lack of variety in sentence structure
awk	awkward
#	insert space
‿	close up space
num	error in use of numbers
⟳→	move
∾	transpose or switch

Adapted from *Exploring Writing in the Content Areas* by Maria Carty

8 Types of Essays

Get back, Loretta!

In my years as a Language Arts teacher, I spent most of my time teaching Grade 5 in elementary schools, and Grade 8 and 9 in junior high or middle schools. The two most common types of essays were personal essays and persuasive essays.

The Personal Essay

In my definition, a personal essay explains an issue that a student feels strongly about, or talks about a topic that is of interest to the student. Whether an issue or a topic, some research is expected. Technically, these might be referred to as research essays.

It's not difficult to talk about something that you are interested in or feel strongly about. To write about a topic of interest should be relatively easy as well. The trick is to get your students to find a topic that truly holds interest for them and then to commit to writing about it in an essay.

A teacher I know and admire—we'll call him Ted—asked his class to write in their journals about an issue or topic they felt strongly about. It was an open-ended request: no lengthy discussion, no suggested list. These are some of the issues/topics that resulted:

- Divorce: Its Effects on Children
- Poverty
- Hockey is the greatest sport in the world
- Labeling
- Hypocrisy and Government
- The Horror of Meningitis
- We need a recreational facility, especially a swimming pool, at this end of town.

Journal writing allowed the students to explore inner thoughts and feelings about the issue. Some venting ensued, some wandering around and exploring took place, some clarification occurred, and, as always, more questions arose.

The students now had a purpose—to explain their particular issue. They were given a choice as to how to share their feelings: either write an essay or write an essay (remember, this is a true story). Being in Grade 8, they weren't totally familiar with the genre so Ted went through the "What is an Essay?" routine with them (see Chapter 1).

The same students who were usually slower than a turtle climbing a steep hill dragging a piano into a headwind were the same students who couldn't wait to get started actually writing the essay. It was, "No outline for me, Teacher Man. Let's get this show on the road. Get back, Loretta, I'm ready to write." I would like to say that after Ted gave them a "Plan Your Work and Work Your Plan" chat, these overzealous authors understood the error of their enthusiasm and agreed to work smarter and not harder. They didn't.

The next step was to create an outline for each student that included the ideas the student wanted to appear in the essay. Some of the ideas were already in place because of the journal writing. Some ideas had arisen because of the questions that surfaced during the writing process.

Ted assigned the writing of an initial outline—but only for the body of the essay. The introductory and concluding paragraphs could be added later (see Chapter 6).

The next step (or "Number Next" as I used to say) was to create a more detailed outline. The plan was to get the students to create the basis, the framework, for an essay in point form. When they

1. found the answers to the questions that had arisen, and
2. added the details that were missing,

they were ready to reconsider the order of their ideas. They were at the "Add, Delete, Rearrange" part of essay building (see Revising, pages 75–80, for specific suggestions).

Ted had them do an exercise in which they considered by themselves, and then with one another,

- Should anything be added?
- Should anything be deleted?
- Are the ideas arranged in the most effective order?

With the answers to these questions, the students were able do a written copy of their essays. Without going into laborious explanation, I can state the class continued and completed the essay assignment. As literary compositions, the results varied considerably.

I believe that one of the most important things about this assignment was the students' ability to choose a topic of personal interest. Ted gave his students an opportunity. The girl who wrote about getting a swimming pool in her end of the city was able to vent some very strong feelings, as was the girl who had been affected by divorce…and on it went.

Teaching Tip
- If you are at the stage where your students are not familiar with essay writing, I would highly recommend the personal essay as a first step.

The Persuasive Essay

It has occurred to me, on occasion, to give up teaching. The dilemma: what would I do? Go into sales? Get paid in relation to how hard I worked? Interesting concept. What would I sell? Whatever it was, I would have to believe in it totally, so that I could sell it with gusto, with enthusiasm unbridled by any fear that I wasn't doing the potential buyer anything but a favor.

The persuasive essay provides a wonderful opportunity for the student author to be a salesperson, to choose a product (an idea) and convince the reader to buy it. To be able to convince someone to do something, to change a point of view, puts the author in a position of power. This is appealing to many.

The teacher's job is to persuade students that there is such a thing as the Power of One. Part of the challenge is addressed when students know that their essays are headed for a real audience and not just the teacher's marking pile. The student must first decide what point to make, what point of view the reader will adopt, what action should result because of the essay.

I have hauled out the somewhat timeworn list of possibilities:

Curfews	School uniforms	Capital punishment
Driving age	Euthanasia	Animal testing
School dress code	Abortion	Age discrimination

I am sure that you can add to this list of usual suspects. At least, it's a starting point. A good brainstorming session usually provides a sufficient list. The critical element is to get the right topic for the right student—something that the student shows an interest in.

I have found that students, once they have a topic and point of view that they wish to defend, almost automatically go into *plus and minus* mode, or *advantage and disadvantage* listing, that is, once they can stand back enough to see that there may be more than one side to the issue. There's more to making a convincing argument than pointing out the two sides of an issue.

Part of our curriculum was, then wasn't, now is again a consideration of advertising techniques. What a wonderful way to persuade someone. As a teacher, I needed to make the connection for my students between the unit on Advertising and a persuasive essay. Many of them got the connection.

Common Advertising Techniques.

Bandwagon: "Everyone else is doing it. Don't be left out. Get on the bandwagon!"

Testimonial: An authority or a well-known person states that the product is good.

Scientific Approach: Most people are awed by science. If something sounds scientific, it seems more believable.

Transfer: We transfer our feelings about one thing to something else. If a politician stands in front of our country's flag, we associate our feelings of patriotism with the person.

Glittering Generalities: We baffle our readers with glowing terms that don't really have any substance.

Plain Folks: Down-to-earth, ordinary people seem more believable. We accept what they say, just as we accept advice from a grandma.

Snob Appeal: Many people are attracted to things associated with the rich and famous.

Essays are not television ads. At the same time, I think we do a disservice to our students if we don't remind them that selling is selling, and offer them the opportunity to integrate what they know about the techniques of advertising into swaying or convincing their readers as they write their persuasive essays.

If the personal essay appeals to the student who strongly feels the need to explain an issue or who feels the need to learn more about a topic of interest, the persuasive essay appeals to the competitive student because it's a contest.

I have had the most success when I compare a persuasive essay to an argument or a debate. With students in their early teens, I often suggest that there is an upcoming party that they want to attend. I ask how they would convince their parents to allow them to go. I warn them that parents are not going to be convinced after hearing only the positive side. Parents will have questions. Are the students prepared to respond? Mom or Dad will not be happy if their child cannot provide answers. The trick is for students to think about what their parents will say and what they will say in response. It's a bit like preparing an effective lesson plan. The experienced teacher always asks, "So where can things go wrong? What can I do to avoid the problems?" If you have done any debating with your students, they should be able to argue from both sides.

I always begin a look at persuasive essays with an anticipatory set that consists of two utterances:

> *Are you here to do something, or are you here for something to do?*
> and
> *Get back, Loretta!*

The first is my challenge to my students to stand for something. Inquiring minds will question the second statement. As teachers, we often have little sayings that we repeat under certain circumstances. "Get back, Loretta!" is what I say whenever it's time to get work, to get into high gear. Anyone in the way is in danger of being bowled over as action is about to begin. I guess you have to be there.

A Final Word: Celebrate

"Let the bells ring out and the banners fly. Your essay is fantabulous. Let's have a party!" Exclamations like these are rarely heard upon the completion of an essay. Okay—they're *never* heard.

In my last three years of teaching, I promised myself that I would do my utmost to make those years the very best ones of my career. One of the beautiful things about teaching is that you get to start fresh each year. For the 28 preceding years, I had always ended the term with a promise: "Next year, I'll get it right." Well, I had only three more chances.

One of the things that I needed to get right was the celebrating of student work. Too often, by the time it came to celebrate, everyone was too pooped to pop, too tired to tango. My first pledge was to have student work published in our monthly school newsletter—and I kept that promise. Newsletters don't lend themselves to the publication of entire pieces of student work, so I often selected parts. For essays, an interesting introduction works well for publication, as does a good body paragraph. And to those who post lengthy editions of student work on bulletin boards, I hope you are doing it for the aesthetic value because I have never read anything of length on a bulletin board. Have you?

I would like to say that my last three years saw a number of other celebrations for the essay. They didn't. Even when it was a priority, and even when I reduced my teaching load so that I could enjoy my final year with a prep period each and every day, I was still unable to accomplish all that I wanted. Welcome to teaching.

On my wish list was the concept of putting student writing into the offices of local doctors, dentists, and the like. I know that I would certainly read student work instead of a magazine while I waited in the outer sanctum. The only booklets of student work I can claim to have worked on were a series of poetry anthologies that find infrequent (but occasional) readership in our school library.

Another opportunity involves exemplars, a solid and viable way to celebrate the essay. An exemplary essay can be a shining example as a whole. It is also possible for an essay to contain exemplary parts—kind of like people. If I were looking for a hallway display during essay time, it would be the good parts that would go up for viewing.

Showing growth is yet another method of celebration, and the portfolio of student work presents this opportunity. There used to be a T-shirt line that had a slogan, "Second place is the first loser," and, sadly, our society seems to have embraced this philosophy. I prefer to celebrate even small victories. When contrasted against an earlier work, whether it is an essay or some other piece of prose, the current effort will likely indicate that progress has been made.

Portfolios require a system in place to collect student work. My method was relatively simple: provide each student with a file folder, purchase a file holder from a office supply store (or cover a detergent box with MacTac), have dividers within the folder holder for easy dissemination and collection of the folders, and finally, clear out the folders at every opportunity.

The school where I completed my full-time teaching career held student-led conferences each spring. The teacher chose assignments for a student to show his or her parents, and then the student got to choose several assignments to share. The whole system of student-led conferences and sharing student work with parents is an excellent one.

Waiting for a spring conference to share student work with parents while they are in the school is not necessary. I enjoyed some success by sending student work home immediately upon completion. In its simplest form, all that was required was a signature from the parent. In more complicated versions, some sort of comment was required. But the point is that a student's efforts were celebrated, not merely marked and filed.

Writing a good essay is a lot of work. The intrinsic reward is important. Nevertheless, if it's true that the most sincere compliment you can pay is attention, I would hope that you take opportunity to compliment your students by celebrating their efforts.

Bibliography

Abrams, M.H. *A Glossary of Literary Terms.* 6th ed. Fort Worth, TX: Harcourt Brace, 1993.

Armstrong, Tricia *Information Transformation.* Markham, ON: Pembroke, 2003.

Carty, Maria *Exploring Writing in the Content Areas.* Markham, ON: Pembroke, 2005.

Caviglioli, Oliver and Ian Harris *Thinking Visually.* Markham, ON: Pembroke, 2003.

Foster, Graham *Seven Steps to Successful Writing.* Markham, ON: Pembroke, 2004.

Gregory, Kathleen, Caren Cameron, and Anne Davies *Setting and Using Criteria.* Courtenay, BC: Connections Publishing, 1997.

Gregory, Kathleen, Caren Cameron, and Anne Davies *Self-Assessment and Goal-Setting.* Courtenay, BC: Connections Publishing, 2000.

Gregory, Kathleen, Caren Cameron, and Anne Davies *Conferencing and Reporting.* Courtenay, BC: Connections Publishing, 2001.

Hall, Donald "A Sense of Story" *Voices in the Middle* September 2003, 8-14.

Harvey, Stephanie *Nonfiction Matters.* Portland, ME: Stenhouse, 1998.

Hunter, Madeline *Mastery Teaching: Increasing Instructional Effectiveness in Secondary Schools, Colleges, and Universities.* El Segundo, CA: TIP Publications, 1982.

Koechlin, Carol and Sandi Zwaan *Info Tasks for Successful Learning.* Markham, ON: Pembroke, 2001.

Kohn, Alfie "The Trouble with Rubrics" *English Journal,* March 2006 http://www.alfiekohn.org/teaching/rubrics.htm

Parsons, Les *Revising & Editing.* Markham, ON: Pembroke, 2001.

Portalupi, JoAnn and Ralph Fletcher *Nonfiction Craft Lessons.* Portland, ME: Stenhouse, 2001.

Sichel, Martin "Abrupt Climate Change" Taped conversation, October 2006.

Tate, Marcia L. *Reading and Language Arts Worksheets Don't Grow Dendrites: 20 Literacy Strategies That Engage the Brain.* Thousand Oaks, CA: Corwin Press, 2005.

Twain, Mark *The Adventures of Tom Sawyer.* Pleasantville, NY: Houghton Mifflin, 1985.

Whitehead, David *Writing Frameworks.* Markham, ON: Pembroke, 2003.

Wormeli, Rick *Fair Isn't Always Equal: Assessing & Grading in the Differentiated Classroom.* Portland, ME: Stenhouse, 2006.

Index